Distillation of Sound

Dub and the Creation of Culture

Distillation of Sound

Dub and the Creation of Culture

Eric Abbey

Bristol, UK / Chicago, USA

First published in the UK in 2022 by
Intellect, The Mill, Parnall Road, Fishponds, Bristol, BS16 3JG, UK

First published in the USA in 2022 by
Intellect, The University of Chicago Press, 1427 E. 60th Street, Chicago, IL 60637, USA

Copyright © 2022 Intellect Ltd

All rights reserved. No part of this publication may be reproduced, stored in a retrieval system, or transmitted, in any form or by any means, electronic, mechanical, photocopying, recording, or otherwise, without written permission.

A catalogue record for this book is available from the British Library.

Copy editor: MPS Limited
Cover designer: Tanya Montefusco
Layout designer: Aleksandra Szumlas
Production editor: Sophia Munyengeterwa
Typesetter: MPS Limited

Cover image: Stack of 45 rpm records at Rocker's International Record store on Orange Street in Kingston, JA. Photo courtesy of Cassandra Abbey.

Paperback ISBN: 978-1-78938-539-7
ePDF ISBN: 978-1-78938-540-3
ePUB ISBN: 978-1-78938-541-0

Printed and bound by Short Run.

To find out about all our publications, please visit our website. There you can subscribe to our e-newsletter, browse or download our current catalogue, and buy any titles that are in print.

www.intellectbooks.com

This is a peer-reviewed publication.

*To Cassandra, Owen, Brendan, Aiden,
Greyson and Chase: Forward*

Contents

Acknowledgements — ix
Preface — xi
Introduction — xiii

Chapter 1 — 1
Version and Dub: The Distinction Within Reggae

Chapter 2 — 17
Java, Java, Java, Java and *Aquarius Dub*:
The Start of a Culture

Chapter 3 — 39
Blackboard Jungle Dub and the Splicing of Culture

Chapter 4 — 55
The Message Spreads: Prince Buster and
the Sound of Jamaica

Chapter 5 — 71
How It All Began: King Tubby and the
Sound of Dub

Chapter 6 — 89
The New Sound: England and the Spread
of Culture

Chapter 7 — 109
Dub in New York City and the Hip Hop Generation

Chapter 8
Japan and the Rising Sound of Dub   133

Chapter 9
Distillation of Sound   149

Endnotes   161
References   163
About the Author   171
Index   173

Acknowledgements

This project would not have been possible without the support of the people in my life. Thank you to everyone who has ever played a role. To Owen and Brendan for being my hooligans. To Cassandra for allowing me to feel the peace that was needed to complete this project and for always supporting me and being my Queen. To Aiden, Chase and Greyson for letting me be a part of their lives. To Jeremy Abbey for the constant push. To everyone at Eastern Kendo Club for understanding my absence while working on this project. To Oakland Community College for giving me a chance to teach and research. To everyone at Wayne State University, from my cohort that helped me through the course work, to the professors who took the time to read and critique my work. To Dr. Steven Shaviro and Dr. Jonathan Flatley for inspiration and guidance. To Dr. Tom Kitts for always being a mentor and friend. To Dr. Evan Ware for the inspiration to finish the project as well. To Dr. Sonjah Stanley-Niaah and everyone at the University of the West Indies for their time and conversation. To all the interview subjects that took the time to speak with me for this book. All these people have been a major part of this project, and it would not have been possible to write without them.

    Others have also played a role in my life during this time, most importantly Charlie Kondek and Zakiah Philips for the help running the club and for always being great friends to me. To the Popular Culture Association for giving me a platform to present ideas to others. To my editors and others who worked on the book at Intellect. To the people that I play music and travel with, you always make the drama disappear. To the Jamaican musicians and engineers who created a music that inspired and motivated me to write. To the people still performing reggae, rocksteady, ska and dub music around the world. Thank you.

Preface

Jamaican music has always been about creating with what is at hand. Taking what is around you and making it into something great is the key to dub and Jamaican culture. This attitude is what this project is about. There is not enough written on the music that has inspired and influenced so many people around the world, and this is an addition to the conversation. Dub music fixates on the engineer as a musician and, in doing so, allows for the creator to interact with technology. Through this, the mixing board and other electronic elements become musical instruments. Now, these technologies are dominant in contemporary music and allow for people to easily create in their own homes. Without the engineers and musicians in the following work, these changes and shifts in technology and music would not have occurred.

Dub is also a refiguring of already existing music. What this demonstrates is that music is ever evolving and can be shifted through technology. It also suggests that recorded music can always be modified and expanded upon. In our contemporary world, this modification is seen every day online and in people's daily lives. Dub created a way to view these changes through music. The influence of technology in the development of culture is the key to this work and our development in society. How technology can be modified, changed and evolved through the interaction of the engineer is the focus of this project. Hopefully, this work will further the importance of dub music and culture in our society. The definition and distinction between version and dub are also an important element in the following work. Jamaican music needs to be discussed more for its influence and creative force in the entirety of the music world.

Introduction

Dub is a post-production thing. The engineer, the one who understands how electricity works and moves through the board that can bring forth sound out of the board as it is an instrument.
  Janine Elizabeth Cunningham (aka Jah 9) (2019)

Dub music in Jamaica started in the early 1970s and by the end of the decade had influenced an entire population. The music began to use the rhythm track of a song as a song itself and spread quickly throughout the sound systems[1] of the island. The importance of dub music and its influence on the music world frames this work. Dub music fixates on different elements that form and describe this culture. The other main points of discussion here relate to the separation between dub as a product and dub as an act of the engineer. Codifying these two elements, and tracing them, will allow for a more definitive approach to the culture and music of dub. To define it, and its surrounding elements, five of the first albums produced in the genre are discussed in three parameters that help to define and set up the culture of dub music. How dub travelled and distilled to three places in the world is then discussed with a focus on New York City, England and Japan. The term culture is used heavily throughout history in different ways. For this work, I will be focusing on culture as discussed by Raymond Williams (1976) when he states:

> It is then necessary, he argued, in a decisive innovation, to speak of 'cultures' in the plural: the specific and variable cultures of different nations and periods, but also the specific and variable cultures of social and economic groups within a nation.
>   (51)

The parameters for the culture of dub music are specific and variable and relate to the production of the music and how the sound was constructed and deconstructed through the mixing board. Norman Stolzoff (2000) discusses the reflections of culture and

Distillation of Sound

states: 'We can see, as Bourdieu asserts, that "the most disputed frontier of all is the one which separates the field of cultural production and the field of power" (1993: 43)' (Stolzoff 2000: 18).

The separation between cultural production and the field of power is important in the development of dub and reggae culture in Jamaica. It also demonstrates the difficulties of the distillation of sound throughout the world. Issues arise in terms of assimilation and cultural boundaries when Jamaican music spreads to places like England, Japan, America and other parts of the world. The shift that occurred in the 1960s on how we view and discuss media with Marshall McLuhan's *Understanding Media* (1964) also plays a role in the development of culture through music. He emphasised the split between production and power stating:

> This is merely to say that the personal and social consequences of any medium – that is, of any extension of ourselves – result from the new scale that is introduced into our affairs by each extension of ourselves, or by any new technology.
>
> (McLuhan 1964: 7)

Figure 0.1: Mixing desk at Anchor Studios/Music Works in Kingston, JA. Photo: Courtesy of Cassandra Abbey (2019).

The new technology that was incorporated into music with the invention and use of the mixing console led to the development of dub and furthered reggae music.

With dub, the mixing board became an extension of self beyond what McLuhan suggested since the engineers were inserting themselves directly into the mix. Thus, the boundaries between media and culture significantly changed. Veit Erlmann (2004) states:

> It is now becoming increasingly clear not only that the boundaries between the spoken and written word were much more fluid than McLuhan imagined but also that they were blurred by a host of factors such as class position, ethnicity, and geographic location.
> (17)

With the expansion of these factors, dub became a representation of Jamaican culture through the media that was used to create it.

Williams (1976) furthers the above definition by stating that the third use of the word culture refers to, '[...]the independent and abstract noun which describes the works and practices of intellectual and especially artistic activity. This seems often now the most widespread use; **culture** is music, literature, painting and sculpture, theater and film' (Williams 1976: 52, original emphasis). In this sense, the music of dub is enough to define a culture, but the surrounding elements affected by the creation of this music form a much larger definition. The creation of dub and the version track, both as product and act of the engineer, influenced the sound system and DJ culture of Jamaica. It expanded throughout the world and influenced all forms of electronic music including hip-hop. The distinct nature of dub music, its production and distribution, led to its rareness within the society and formed the artistic elements of this culture.

I will first discuss the differences between version and dub, with a section on foundation riddims[2] and their links to the community, and then continue with a focus on full-length records of dub music. Full-length records are analysed in each section track by track for specific elements that created a distillation of sound throughout the world. The decision to focus on full-length records is due to the important difference that occurred when the entire record was a dub record. A single, or 45 rpm, record is a single statement that has been left out of this discussion to focus on these full-length statements. The determining markers for each track are put forward to link these elements to one another and to demonstrate how this distillation occurred and how it was then transferred to the community. The conclusion of this work shows that dub was formed into a culture through the engineers and producers. This culture was then distilled throughout the world and carries on today because of them.

In this work are sections titled Social and Completion as well. In the sections labelled Social is a discussion on how the surrounding social changes that were happening affected and influenced each record and led to the cultural development of dub. There are many social influences that were paramount in this development, and this work discusses how these directly shaped the surrounding musicians, engineers and producers. The section labelled Completion is the final section in the discussion of each record and aims to bring together the analysis on the individual songs and tracks.

Through the development of recording technologies, the cultural history of reggae and dub music was changed. Once, the artists were simply captured onto the recorded tape and then mixed to preserve the sound. Now, the altered music gave the engineer presence and creative avenues of expression. Jonathan Sterne (2003), in *The Audible Past*, suggests: 'Technologies are repeatable social, cultural, and material processes crystallized into mechanisms' (8). Through the mechanism of the mixing desk and recording technologies, the engineers and producers were brought to the forefront. 'Their mechanical character, the ways in which they commingle physics and culture, can tell us a great deal about the people who build and deploy them' (Sterne 2003: 8). These technological developments created ways in which people who were not musicians could manipulate and control sound and culture.

Thomas Vendrys (2015) also discusses these elements and states: 'Thus, dubs were primarily characterized by a rendering, and even an emphasis, of three traits of their musical material: low-frequency rhythms, syncopation, and rawness' (14). The following albums illustrate these three traits and form a case study on the culture of dub music. Vendry's traits are a starting point in analysis and are expanded and labeled here as the following: timbre, rhythmic interplay and re-production. The albums following represent the ways that dub music formed a culture that influenced the world through these three elements.

A cultural need resonated throughout the community and became linked within the mindset of the people of Jamaica. The three traits of the dub track that formed a culture specifically make up the signs of dub music. With the mixing board, engineers and producers manipulated tracks in ways that significantly define dub music. In *Music as Social Life: The Politics of Participation*, Thomas Turino (2008) suggests:

> Iconic and especially indexical signs tie us to actual experiences, people, and aspects of the environment. Indices are *of* our lives and experiences and thus are potentially invested with greater feeling and senses of intimacy and reality. Indexical experience plus a perception of iconic similarity with other people and forms of life is the basis for feeling direct *empathic connection*.
>
> (16, emphasis added)

This created a connection between the engineers and the mixing board and began the formation of dub music.

The connection between the mixing board, the frequencies of sound and the people became the link that dub created. Through the manipulation of sound, the 'indexical experience' took place and the people moved with the music. This also allowed for the people of Jamaica and around the world to become linked to each other through an empathic modality. This began with the manipulation and control of sound.

Dub begins when engineer Hedley Jones returns from the war. As an electrical engineer and radio operator, he was schooled in the many ways that sound could be manipulated. In 'A history of dub music', Clinton Hutton (2018) states:

> The building of the dub complex begins with the innovations of Hedley Jones who uses his creativity, knowledge, and expertise in music, electronics, and radar technology and operations, to revolutionize sound amplification and audio frequency into distinctive bass, mid-range, and high range.
>
> (n.pag.)

This separation into different tones started a revolution in sound and led to Jones building one of the first well-known studios on the island when he worked with Clement 'Coxsone' Dodd to build Studio One.

In this book, the term dub distinguishes music and tracks that have been manipulated by the engineer and producer. To 'dub something' means to interact with the tracks of the music and to make changes. This is a process of acting upon something that already exists, and this pre-existence is critical to how dub was received. The riddim production method is different from dub and is the method of reusing the same version of a song with different singers and DJs voicing over the top of it. This method would lead to the creation of what are known as foundation riddims that have travelled throughout the world. The specific version or dub of each of these riddims is not as important to most of the population as is the musical format of the version. This method of production led to many producers gaining fame from artists and musicians without giving them credit or monetary compensation.

This is the other side of the development of dub. The ways that producers attempted to gain more money with the reuse of tracks. In this discussion, I will differentiate the two strains by calling tracks and albums primarily used to gain funding 'versions' and the tracks manipulated as musical idioms 'dubs'. While the end goal was to make money on both, there is a distinct difference between the types of manipulations that occurred. In Jamaica, the culture that developed based on these strains is extremely interesting as it relates to today's music culture. Larisa Kingston Mann (2018), in 'Rude citizenship: Jamaican musical challenges to copyright(ed) culture', states:

> When people record music in Jamaica, they will often press the instrumental of a song on one side and the full song on the other side. When that record goes out into the world, there is the expectation that the instrumental is something that other people are going to use. Therefore, built into this material aspect of the music is the understanding that a work is not fixed, and that people will interact with it.
>
> (n.pag.)

This interaction has become the source of the culture of dub and the many ways that people interact with the track determine its longevity.

The term dub is also associated with the dubplate. A dubplate is the acetate master that must be formed first to create a record. These were often used in studios to compare different mixes of songs before the record was pressed. In Jamaica, they became prized possessions of sound system DJs attempting to get the newest and rarest song to play in the dance hall. These acetate versions would start to deteriorate in quality after the first play, much faster than the vinyl that the record would eventually be produced on. Therefore, these dubplates became part of the immediate sound system culture. They were also usually songs that were not guaranteed to be released. In 'Dubplate culture: Analogue islands in the digital stream', DJ Hype explains: '"It's a way of testing out a song, but the Jamaican Sound system clash culture started using it for more exclusive public performances for a one-off song that no one else has got"' (Bennett 2014: n.pag.). Through the technology of the dubplate, music was able to get into the hands of the DJs much more quickly.

Dub's history is grounded in technology as the original track was already cut into the surface of the dubplate. The engineer was then responsible for manipulating the individual tracks to cut the new dub. Kodwo Eshun (1998) discusses dub in *More Brilliant Than the Sun: Adventures in Sonic Fiction*: 'The mixing desk decomposes The Song, leaving a skeletal ribcage' (63). The destructive nature of this editing is what leads this discussion. Through 'destroying' a musician's voice, or the instrumental tracks, the engineer and producer created something unique and propelled their own voices into the track. This could only occur with the technological apparatus that allowed for it. The mixing console shifted, by accident, to become another musical instrument.

The importance of music and the methodology of working within the recorded track sets dub music into a culture of its own. This was not the ska or rocksteady scene that came before it; this was something different that took place within the recording studio and was shared through the sound system directly for the people to experience. One of the important elements of dub, as a culture, is the sound system and the personal nature of the music. The intent of dub music is to be heard and felt live in the sound system with others dancing and feeling the music as the DJ spins and controls the crowd with the track. This led to the formation of a community surrounding various sound systems and the tracks that they could obtain determined their popularity. Even in contemporary sound systems, the concept of hearing the track live is extremely important.

The culture that developed through these sound systems affected the community and the Jamaican people. The production of the records discussed here allowed for this culture to happen. Without the mixing engineers, producers and the developments that occurred in technology, dub would not have existed, and the formation of this culture would not have happened. The timbre, rhythmic interplay and re-production all happened in the studio. Therefore, dub culture was created, and continues to be created, in a recording studio for the specific purpose of being shared with a live audience. Vendryes (2015) states:

> Mixing dubs from existing tracks thus provided a convenient way for producers to offer selectors a variety of tracks to compose their sets and specific tracks to attract an audience hungry for novelty and variety. So, dub was consubstantial to the emergence of the riddim production method, as it constituted a way to introduce diversified and specific interpretations of rhythmic patterns.
>
> (15)

These interpretations formed a culture surrounding different engineers and sounds.

Versioning stems from the genres before dub was created in Jamaica. Ska and rocksteady music began to be versioned when two-track and eventually four-track recorders were invented and came to the island. By recording the musicians on three of the tracks and the vocalists on the last remaining one, the producers found that they could easily create a B-side to a record with the instrumental version of the song. This technique went on to become versioning and dub, and the technology that allowed for this to occur was imperative to this development.

The people interacting with the work were also important to dub and reggae culture. As stated by Mann previously, Jamaican music contains an understanding that the work is not a fixed element. This becomes extremely problematic when discussing copyright issues and performer's rights, but it is how Jamaican music has transformed the world as well. The concept that a song, version or dub is recorded to be used by others is a part of

Jamaican culture and reggae itself. This also becomes an important part of the distillation of the music to other parts of the world because when the music travels to other parts of the world, it is not used but is reused and mimicked. When dub reaches England, America and Japan, the music is mostly created by musicians to be dubbed, not as reused versions.

The interaction between the track, dubplate and people confirms the notion that music was and is used to create cultures. The class position of the people became extremely important when the sound systems began. The sound systems began as ways to get information to the people. They began as a type of radio station for the people who had no radios. A way for the news of the town and country to reach people who it would normally not reach and a political distribution centre. In *Wake the Town and Tell the People: Dancehall Culture in Jamaica*, Norman Stolzoff (2000) states: 'The sound systems allowed people who were previously excluded because of lower-class standing to enter the field of dancehall promotion. [...] In this sense, the sound systems made dance entertainment widely available to those who were unable to afford it' (42). Without the music being created and controlled in the lower classes, and distributed by them, we would not have access to this culture.

The social class position of the creators of dub was also an important part of the creation of this culture. Errol Thompson, King Tubby, Lee 'Scratch' Perry and others were not part of the upper classes at their start and were all forced to create with technology and machinery that was of their own creation and re-production. This is extremely important in the link between Jamaica and the rest of the world as the distillation of the culture through sound began in the lower classes of Jamaica. These engineers were all using technology that was handed down or borrowed from other producers. They took what they had and made it into something that we still attempt to replicate today.

In today's studios, many people attempt to recreate the 'original' sounds of Jamaica with contemporary technology in many different ways. What is often demonstrated through this attempt is the fact that it was the person behind the technology that made the sound. This is an extremely important part of what happened in Jamaica and how it affected the world. The empathic connection that took place between the engineer and the technology gave dub its founding and sound. You can attempt to recreate the sounds of

Distillation of Sound

King Tubby's studio, but you can never be King Tubby, and this is where, and how, the distillation of sound began.

Dub is a particular cultural referent that developed because of a media interacting with the cultural changes around it. The technology developed in relation to the people and the ways that they gathered in the streets and around the studios. Although this discussion will not get into semiotic theory, Umberto Eco's (1984) work on semiotics and culture is used here as a beginning. In *Semiotics and the Philosophy of Language*, he states:

> Culture, art, language, manufactured objects are phenomena of collective interactions governed by the same laws. Cultural life is not a spontaneous spiritual creation, but rather, is rule-governed. These rules represent an object of investigation, since they probably are something deeper and more universal than their transitory and superficial instantiations.
>
> (Eco 1994: 167)

These 'collective interactions' are what is being discussed throughout this book. To begin, we need to focus on specific traits and how they are manipulated to form a song and then how they influence the culture.

The timbre of dub is one of the main elements in the formation of the track and the culture surrounding it. This timbre is fixated on the bass end of the audio spectrum and is created through various efforts in the studio. By focusing on the bass in the production of dub, the engineers allowed the music to influence the physical body of listeners in the dance hall. Vendryes (2015) states in 'Versions, dubs, and riddims: Dub and the transient dynamics of Jamaican music',

> Jamaican music has then been designed to be felt as much as it is heard, to generate what Henriques calls 'sonic dominance', where 'the bass line beats on our chest, vibrating the flesh, playing on the bone, and resonating the genitals' (2003: 452).
>
> (15)

This feeling of dub is through the timbre of the track, with the bass frequencies taking precedence in the song and album. Other factors influence the timbre of dub culture, but the bass resonance is the most important element in the musical track.

Another way that this lower resonance is achieved in the recording is through the removal and deletion of the higher-end frequencies. With the use of a high-pass and low-pass filter on the mixing board itself and by removing higher-toned instruments like horns, piano and guitar, this is accomplished. Although these instruments are not completely removed, the engineer reconstructs the parts focusing on the lower end sound. This re-production, through removal, is another pivotal part of dub culture and what sets the music apart from other forms of art and culture. By constructing the track around bass tones, the engineer created a significant shift away from the vocal and lead singer versions that had become popular.

The cultural reflections within the dub mix are aggressive and dark. These tonal shifts take the 'happy' sound of reggae and ska and manipulate them into the street sound that was occurring around the engineers at the time. Stolzoff (2000) states: 'The sound system dance, or "blues dance" as it was called, was strictly a downtown phenomenon, which means it attracted black, lower-class people who lived in ghetto areas (Clarke 1980)' (49). The insertion of gunshots and military sirens suggest a militaristic feeling. Tubby and Perry both were instrumental in establishing these shifts in tones and the dub mix grew in relation to the 'war in the streets'. The technology of the mixing board and elements such as reverb and delay allowed this to happen. Richard Burgess (2014), in *The History of Music Production*, suggests: 'The phonograph opened up a new creative medium that allowed the development of the art of music production. Technology is but one of the means to the end of music production, which has many facets' (1). Burgess discusses the record player as a key defining element in music production.

The turntable was a key invention to all of music and when technology allowed for mixing boards to be produced more cheaply, the engineers took hold. What the record player did for music, the mixing board did for reggae and Jamaica. As the technology of the mixing board grew, the studios in Jamaica attempted to keep up with the latest trends. By doing so, the older mixing boards were made available for sale and use by engineers that were not able to afford the top of the line gear. This forced these engineers to be creative and to work with what they had access to, thus leading to dub. What the engineer did with what they had was the most important element in the beginning of this music. Composition of sound is the key to dub.

In the early stages of mixing technology, the engineer determined the output of the recording. The musicians and the original recording itself became secondary and fell to the background of the sound. The engineer became the musician and the manipulation became the song. Thom Holmes (2002), in *Electronic and Experimental Music: Pioneers in Technology and Composition*, suggests: 'In electronic music, sound itself becomes a theme of composition. The ability to get inside the physics of a sound and directly manipulate its characteristics provides an entirely new resource for composing music' (11). It is this 'getting inside' that the dub engineers excelled at and through the manipulation of the track the sound was produced through technology.

Most of the engineers that gave dub its beginnings were electronic engineers first before they sat behind the mixing board. These were people who had extensive knowledge of what electronic waves and sound did in certain configurations. They had experience building and rebuilding speakers, amplifiers and record players before they began working with musical tracks and recordings. This knowledge cannot be overstated as it allowed for them to get 'inside the physics of a sound' and to manipulate that sound. In the interviews and discussions for this book, every engineer stated that this was the difference between them and the studio engineers of today. The first-hand knowledge of the electronics behind the sound led to an understanding that is not often developed today.

King (Prince) Jammy discussed how he began producing records after getting to the Waterhouse area of Kingston and meeting up with Black Uhuru. This was the first album from them *Love Crisis* (1978) on Jammy's Records, which was then changed to *Black Sounds of Freedom* remixed and released on Greensleeves. For Jammy, there are even subsets of dub, like instrumental dub and vocal dub that differ in many ways. He talked about dub stating: 'Dub music is created by the engineer's feelings at the moment that he is mixing' (James 2019). This moment has often shifted based on the technology that was at hand for the engineer to use. This is the connection between the technology and the person, which developed into dub around the world.

The second element of dub culture is the rhythmic interplay and the manipulation of the higher-toned instruments. The incorporation of these sounds, generally, reminds the listener of the original track. The rhythmic interplay originally comes from Nyabinghi drumming, mento and burru music, and Jamaican blues and shuffle. This rhythmic interplay relies on the piano and guitar performing on the upbeat of the music and not the downbeat. This creates a bright and rhythmic pattern based on the feel of the song and not focused on the individual instrument. The rhythmic interplay of dub and Jamaican music uses the guitar and piano as rhythm instruments that align with the drum patterns. This is extremely different from other forms of music where the piano and guitar are heard and viewed as lead instruments. One of the key elements in Jamaican popular music is this rhythmic interplay and how the guitar and piano play similar patterns to the drums.

Re-production is the third area of focus for the determining of dub culture. By the re-production of the track of music, I intend to discuss and demonstrate what specific aspects of the track the engineer and producer have re-produced. This differs from the way that the original track was recorded and performed by the musicians and creates the distinct difference and meaning of dub. Many forms of re-production exist, and they differ from engineer to engineer, but there are commonalities between the methods. The shared elements of the re-production formed the basis of dub culture and shaped its reception. These elements are the use of reverb and delay units, the use of natural or raw sounds in the studio and the removal and insertion of instruments in differing ways.

By using these re-production methods, the engineers added their own style and sound to the recorded track. These differences feature on the albums discussed, and the engineers became well known for them. The ways in which Errol Thompson, King Tubby, Lee 'Scratch' Perry and others re-produced the dub led to a distinct culture. In *Dub: Soundscapes and Shattered Songs in Jamaican Reggae*, Michael Veal (2007) states: 'Under Lee Perry, Errol Thompson, King Tubby, and many others, dub became an art form unto itself, with the composer acting as both deconstructionist and soundscape architect' (94). The use of the mixing board as an instrument in this re-production became central to the idea and sound of dub. What the engineer did with it became their signature and the music itself was secondary to this re-production. The sound had to be right for the audience to get the vibe of the track, but the original recorded track was only audible in parts.

The removal and re-production of the track are what makes dub a sound and a culture. Lou Gooden (2015) suggests:

> The sound of Dub music was also created by means of reconstructing a recording so that snatches of the original tune become rhythmic elements to be played with, chopped up, looped, phased and sprinkled with all manner of sound effects. This was remixing as an end rather than merely the means.
>
> (227)

This remixing was only possible due to the technology that was available and the knowledge of the electronics and sonic values of that technology. The engineers that knew this became just as valuable as the musicians who had recorded on the track.

These three elements make up the culture of dub music and fixate the creation of a song and album into a specific realm. The main purpose of dub was for the sound systems and their use of these songs became a part of this culture as well. The way that each sound system had a relationship with a studio or specific engineer created competition but also curated a sound. The sound system was the reason for the dub. As Paul Sullivan (2014) states: 'The importance of the sound system cannot be understated in the development of dub, not only because of the dissemination of the music but also because of its role in the music's creative evolution' (8). This relationship between the sound system and the engineer allowed the constructive elements to frame the reception of each song.

The sound of dub then began to go through the 'yard', or Jamaican dance halls, and the technology of the record player and the process of mixing the song became dominant. People began to relate certain dubs with certain engineers and even certain effects that each engineer used. Tubby for his use of reverb and delay while Lee 'Scratch' Perry for what he inserted into the mix. With the expansion of the means of distribution and Jamaican music 'breaking through' to other countries with artists like Bob Marley and Peter Tosh, the engineer relegated to the background. Curwen Best (2004) in *Culture @ the Cutting Edge* suggests: 'This is the problematic of technological innovation, and it is also the challenge of economic and cultural development' (150). Due to this shift in popularity, dub music was reverted to the streets and the yard.

There are many writings on the work and effectiveness of Bob Marley on the distillation of Jamaican music throughout the world. Many, including myself, would not know about Jamaican music if it was not for the music of Bob Marley and the Wailers. What occurred to his music when it was obtained in England is a legendary discussion that is held elsewhere. The most important issue, for this work, is that the sound of Jamaica shifted when it was taken to England to what was thought to be a more 'sellable' sound. Here is where the culture of dub transmits to and through the underground to become an even more important part of Jamaica.

By transmitting the dub to the community, the sound systems furthered the culture of dub music and the timbre, rhythmic interplay and re-production of the music became known. These elements allowed the listeners to immerse in the sound. Other elements began to take hold once the record played. Toasting and other forms of manipulation by the DJ were only possible because of the version and dub tracks produced. This toasting would continue throughout the world to become rap and hip-hop in New York. This was possible with the removal of the vocal track in dub and version creation. Without the culture of dub and the technological growth that occurred with the mixing board as an instrument, many musical styles would not exist.

These engineers and producers helped to change the culture that surrounded them through the sounds that they were creating. In many ways, these sounds became the new culture of Jamaica. As Mark Abel (2016) states:

> The suggestion here is the dialectical one that the temporalities of artistic forms do not simply passively reflect social time, whose reality is, in any case, disputable, but through the process of making it visible or explicit, contributes to its re-production in some way.
>
> (12)

Dub producers made the smallest elements of the music appear and manipulated these sounds to affect the way the culture operated.

Cultural connections through sound are the key elements within this book. The ways in which the sound of Jamaica, and particularly dub music, influenced the creation of culture frame this work. Veit Erlmann (2004) suggests:

> The ways in which people relate to each other through the sense of hearing also provide important insights into a wide range of issues confronting societies around the world as they grapple with the massive changes wrought by modernization, technologization, and globalization.
>
> (3)

These ways can be heard in many of the dub records that continue to resonate throughout the world. The records discussed here still play heavy roles in the spread of the culture of dub and allow for us to discuss many issues regarding society.

Focusing on the sound of a culture, and how that sound creates and shapes that culture, is another important point of this book. The sound of dub music changed the ways in which people view the engineer and musicians involved. Throughout the world, the processes associated with dub music can be heard. Even the concept of 'dubbing' something has become associated with changing the original recorded music in any genre. There are many people who consider dub as an act, not as a genre of music, and this is not necessarily wrong. Here, the genre is discussed as an act. The act of manipulating sound can be done to any genre, but it got its start in Jamaica with ska, rocksteady and reggae music.

The concept of sound creating a culture is one that involves the realization that sound is as important, if not more so than sight for thinking about connections in life. Henriques (2011) states: 'This emerges from the intimate nature of the relationship between sound and embodiment, one that is matched by that between vision and the disembodied mind, as an entirely different sensory modality and another kind of object altogether' (xxvii). The object that is created through the embodiment of sound fixates the listener as an entity. Because the sound is structured and formed in a specific way, the engineer takes precedent in this embodiment. It is the intent of the engineer to create a sound that the listener responds to, and it is this response that makes dub such an important part of the development of Jamaican culture.

There are also many issues revolving around the term genre in the study of music, and Jamaican popular music is no different.

For this book, dub is being formally discussed as an act of the engineer and how that engineer inserts themselves into the music, through the mixing board. Simon Frith, in *Performing Rites: On the Value of Popular Music*, states:

> Genre matters remain a matter of elaborate and unresolvable debate. Or, to put this more sensibly, the genre labelling process is better understood as something collusive than as something invented individually, as a result of a loose *agreement* among musicians and fans, writers and discjockeys.
>
> (1996: 88, emphasis added)

The nature of defining dub as a genre must be collusive as the engineer is working with pre-existing material to define and construct a new version of sound.

The intent in this discussion is to demonstrate how we can view dub as the sound of a culture and how these connections were created and transmitted throughout Jamaica and eventually the globe. Julian Henriques (2011), in *Sonic Bodies: Reggae Soundsystems, Performance Techniques, and Ways of Knowing* elaborates and states that:

> Listening concerns depths, rather than surfaces, disposing it to evaluation, as with 'sound judgement,' further than mere monitoring. It is a haptic sense and, as touch itself, simultaneously both makes a connection between one and another, and recognizes their separation.
>
> (xxvii)

The first records produced in the dub style and sound formed a starting point in the creation of a culture. Through thinking through the sound of these albums, we can see how this began and how it continues to influence people and form community.

Chapter 1
Version and Dub: The Distinction Within Reggae

Dub is without any end. It's infinite. It keeps going on and on.
                    Hopeton 'Scientist' Brown (2019)

Within dub music is a distinction that has been argued and shifted since the beginning of the genre. This distinction is between the version, which is a track that has little to no manipulation from the engineer, and the dub, which is manipulated completely. This distinction is due to issues involving copyright, usage and the musicians who have performed on the tracks. It is also important to recognize the ways in which dub music was distilled into England and the shift that occurred there and, elsewhere, with this distinction. When dub arrived in England, the music changed and began to separate into these categories even further. The separation occurs when the music that is recorded is used in different ways. These two usages are called 'version', when the music is reused by the producer for the purpose of getting more out of the original track, with or without the vocalist, and 'dub', when the music is reconstructed by the engineer and becomes a different sounding musical artifact. Both of these strains cross and are called many different things throughout the history of Jamaican music. Some of the nomenclature relates to the distillation throughout the world, while other naming issues occur to avoid copyright and other legal issues.

The main point of the version is to reuse the original music track without the vocal or with the vocal coming in and out of the track.

This allowed the producer of a popular song to put the musical track on the B-side of the single and to get more out of a single recording. Often this was called the version of the song and most often takes place in the early days of ska, rocksteady and reggae. The version can be heard in many places throughout the early 1960s in Jamaica and does not shift into what many call dub until much later. Brent Hagerman (2015), in 'From dub plate to dancehall: Versioning as an analogue template for digital reggae', states:

> Versioning and riddims are the essential tools of this art form in the studio. Since its inception versioning has dictated the mode of creation of reggae songs so that it is standard practice for a singer or deejay to write a new song using a pre-recorded backing track, or a riddim, as opposed to writing an autonomous stand-alone composition.
>
> (130)

This concept begins with the invention of multi-track recorders.

Figure 1.1: DJ set up at Tony Meyer's yard in Kingston, JA. Photo: Courtesy of Cassandra Abbey (2019).

Version and Dub

With the invention of multi-track recording, the engineer could record the musicians on one track and the vocalists on another. As the track count increased with the technology, the musicians were given multiple tracks, and the vocalists were then overdubbed or relegated to one track. The technology dictated this shift to versioning and the producers realizing that they could simply release the song without the vocal on the B-side of the record led to versioning, foundation riddims and eventually dub.

The argument here is that these versions were the first types of dub music and, if the engineer moved faders and added elements to the track, it was not as often or as much as in later years. The version also allowed the musicians to be heard and to become the focus of the song. By removing the vocal, the musicians were the focus of the version, and this is why it was often called a version of the song. The process of versioning in a specific way comes later when discussing the music.

The DJ in the sound system would often use this version as a way to talk over the main song that was just played. The main example of this is the start of DJ culture with U-Roy, Big Youth and others. The rhythm track gained popularity as the DJ version in the dance hall. This distinction is important as the version was not manipulated nearly as much as a dub in later dub culture in order to allow for the DJ to be present.

The version is also important to discuss in the ways that the music is used by the producers to make money off the same recording. When this was discovered, many producers began versioning songs, and the purely musical track often became more popular than the vocal track. The production of music in all forms was and is about money as the end goal, but this realization that the same song could be sold more than once opened a new market in Jamaica. Hagerman (2015) states:

> This practice of releasing a new version of an older song became known as 'versioning'. For example, in 1968 Toots and the Maytals and Marcia Griffiths had hits ('54–46' and 'Feel Like Jumping', respectively) based on the Ethiopians' 1967 classic 'Train to Skaville'.
> (130)

There are multiple issues with this in terms of payment to musicians and who owns the song that was produced. Many of these issues are still being debated in court, and they are all discussed throughout Jamaica and the world.

The distinction of a version is also important when looking closely at the differences in the musicianship in the studio. For many people, these differences are the key to the different versions and how they sound and feel. Rowan Oliver (2017) states:

> This 'versioning' strategy is useful for the purposes of rhythm section analysis, because the detailed nuances in particular instrumental voices which can often be obscured in the full mix are sometimes more clearly revealed in alternative versions, particularly when the deconstructive techniques of dub mixing have been applied.
>
> (200)

For Oliver, this concept of versioning becomes important when discussing groove-based empathy and other forms of feel.

Oliver's discussion on an 'empathically attuned rhythm section' becomes interesting here not only in the discussion of dub as a whole but also in how the sound was distilled throughout Jamaica. Without this attunement, the track would not be able to have been manipulated as easily by the engineer, and the rhythm track would not have allowed for the DJs to voice over and the versions to occur. The version then becomes something more focused on the musicianship then on what the engineer did to the track.

The musicianship during the ska and rocksteady eras of Jamaica was outstanding with many players coming from the Alpha Boys School. This school was started by nuns of the Sisters of Mercy sect of Catholicism and still carries on today with the mission to encourage young men to be positive members of society. Sister Mary Ignatius Davies was the inspiration for Jamaican music's beginnings with the first sound system being credited to her known as Mutt and Jeff. Musicians such as Don Drummond, Rico Rodriquez, Tommy McCook, Lester Sterling, Johnny 'Dizzy' Moore, Vin Gordon, Leroy Smart, Leroy 'Horsemouth' Wallace, Yellowman and many others attended the school and learned music there. This school saw the foundation of Jamaican music begin and encouraged boys to follow their path to become professional musicians. Without Alpha Boys School and these original musicians, all of Jamaican popular music would have been different.

The musicians and playing style are what became the important part of the version on the B-side of these original records. Without a solid rhythm track, played extremely well, with Jamaican style and focus, the DJs would not have been able to perform in the ways that they did. These musicians also created songs and tracks that were easily changeable by the engineer because of their clarity and power in the rhythm section with the bass and drums. All of the elements discussed throughout this book would not have been possible without the strength of the musicianship.

In most forms of early Jamaican music, the way the music was recorded was very limited in technology. One microphone in the room and a small mixing board were the only ways of capturing these sounds available at the time. This forced the musicians to perform perfectly together without the ability to overdub or recut something that would happen with the advancement of recording technologies. Because of the limited number of tracks on a recorder, the engineer had to use each track to the fullest and then record over the same track with the vocals or other additional sounds. The version is the recording before these additions. Often, these versions would be discarded, but when the song was a hit, the producer would then release these earlier versions as dubs or instrumental versions. This was the first form of dub and what is called here a version.

Technology was important in both avenues of dub, versioning and dub, as the engineer became the artist. The use of what was available to the engineer, and what they did with this technology became central to Jamaican music. With the introduction of the Fairlight mixing console, Jamaican producers were more inclined to stick with the MCI board that they had already, instead of investing in the newest board. This concept of using what you have is significant to the development of Jamaican music. Ray Hitchins (2018) states: 'Technology shapes how music is made, but we also direct how technology evolves' (Hitchins 2018). This is an extremely important part of the culture of dub. Using what is at hand to create new sounds for the sound systems and market defines dub culture.

Directing how technology evolves becomes relevant when looking at the original empathic connection with sound that these engineers, musicians and producers had. They drove the limited technology that was around them to certain points, sometimes even breaking them on purpose to get a specific sound. This was similar to some other recording studios around the world, but in Jamaica, these strategies became fixed modes of recording and shifted the culture. The feeling between the engineer and the technology is the key here. Determining how to use what was at hand led to the development and change of Jamaican popular music.

    Clement Dodd acquired a two-track Ampex recorder in 1964, and this began the change in Jamaican recording. Dodd realized that you could record the rhythm tracks and then record over them as many times as needed to get a layered sound. This led to experimenting with new sounds and filters that would later become important parts of dub. In 1971, King Tubby was at the controls of an MCI JH-400 mixing board allowing him full control of the mix. These two key technological pieces changed the way that Jamaicans recorded and used music. The ability to layer and control the mix were the key ingredients in this shift.

    As time progressed, and technology became more available, the engineers in Jamaica began to insert themselves into the music. This is where the concept of dub gets its start and what many people define as dub, the manipulation of a pre-existing recording by the engineer. Oliver (2017) again makes a distinction,

> the role of the dub mixer relies on an additional, third process of empathy, in which a technological manipulation is artfully applied to the groove factors in existing recordings in order to extract alternative or hidden feeling from within a song, and then communicate this to the listener.
>
> (208)

This technological manipulation is what defines the song as a dub.

    An early example of this would be Errol Thompson's work on the *Dub Serial* record by Joe Gibbs & the Professionals. David Katz (2019) states: 'Those dubs, they just have such textural depth. He was such a phenomenal engineer with exceptional skills, oftentimes overlooked'. Thompson was a part of the interchange and switch to dub and worked on many rhythm versions. Sylvan Morris at Harry J's and Studio One was another pivotal engineer during the early times of dub who worked with versions and eventually crafted dubs.

Sylvan Morris worked with many of the top artists of the original Jamaican sound. He began his career at WIRL radio station and then Treasure Isle studios before landing at Studio One and finally Harry J's. Morris was another example of an engineer who knew electronics and had learned how to build amplifiers before getting behind a mixing board. At Treasure Isle, he mixed the 1967 festival song 'Ba Ba Boom' by the Jamaicans. After leaving Byron Lee at Treasure Isle, he went to work for Coxsone at Studio One. At Studio One, Morris recorded the Heptones and Delroy Wilson and stated to Angus Taylor (2019) in an interview for *Reggaeville*,

> I don't know if you listen to most of them tunes you hear, they have a delay. The Heptones and Delroy Wilson. I used to feedback the output into the input, and you had a delay system. At that time, that was considered to be very revolutionary.
>
> (n.pag.)

When Morris got to Harry J's, after 'Liquidator' had taken off and Chris Blackwell had become involved, dub had just begun.

Morris worked on three full length dub albums at Harry J's, *Dubwise: Morris on Dub* and *Reggae Workshop* in 1975 and *Cultural Dub* in 1978. He discussed cutting dubplates for sound systems and stated to Taylor (2019): 'So we might give one with the pure rhythm and thing and we might give one with a little drum and thing, so the drum and bass thing started' (n.pag.). He continued to work at Harry J's and recorded Bob Marley and the Wailers' *Rastaman Vibration* with Errol Thompson engineering as well.

Thompson and Morris were two of the first engineers to create versions that would eventually turn into dub plates, specials and then dub. The amount of Jamaican music that these two engineers were involved with is immense, and they are both founding members of the sound of Jamaica and the empathic connections that were developed between the mixing board and the people. From here, the version shifted and changed into different areas of Jamaican culture.

An example of the importance of working with the technology is Hopeton Overton Brown, also known as Scientist, the lead engineer at Channel One who worked with King Tubby and Prince Jammy and influenced the entire style of Jamaican music with his recording techniques. As a founding father of Jamaican music, Scientist became disillusioned with the record companies in Jamaica and moved out to further distill the sound in the 1980s. 'I am the one who developed that technology, that style, that way to get all those drums to sound big and fat, coming from Channel One. And then I took it to Tuff Gong' (Brown 2019). The technology that Scientist was responsible for developing in the studio is what led to the distinction between version and dub.

Scientist claims, in multiple interviews, that the reason that dub exists is because of his influence. This contrasts what others say about Sylvan Morris and Errol Thompson and is a typical debate held in Jamaica and around the world. This also suggests that he, as the engineer, begins the manipulation of sound that would become dub music. He tells a story of the different mixing board controls in an interview with Stephen Cooper (2018) for *Reggae Vibes*, '"See this button right here Willie Lindo?" They had been mixing Bob Marley, everybody's song in "monitor mode." [...] Because I'm an electronics engineer, I know how to manage a console' (n.pag.). The simple act of changing the settings on the mixing console is here claimed as the beginning of dub and the creation of a new sound at Tuff Gong. The importance of the engineer is highlighted by Scientist and his use and manipulation of the technology at hand.

Another important statement about dub, and both the version and dub qualifications, is the effectiveness of the musicians playing during the recording. Without solid musicianship and creative songwriting, dub would not have been able to be created. Scientist again states: 'The two things that work hand in hand is the musical composition, the talent of the musician, and the engineer technology that I brought to the studio' (Brown 2019). This combination is pivotal to both avenues of creation.

The way that dub music was and is created forms the basis of this distinction. To define dub as the manipulation of a pre-existing song by the engineer and/or producer is paramount to this discussion as well. The music had to be recorded first and, with people like Morris, Thompson, and Scientist at the mixing board, the original sounds of dub were captured. Musicians like Flabba Holt, bassist from Roots Radics and studio musician and Sly and Robbie Shakespeare were the key players in this genre and created the feel and music that became dub. The rhythm had to be there before the engineer could do anything to the track.

I am distinguishing this nomenclature from the often-used concept of riddim in reggae circles as a version of the song that is known and becomes a signature through the bass and drum parts. This is where the distillation of sound takes prominence as well. A riddim, in most cases, is a signature track as Henriques states: 'Often described as "foundation riddims," recognizing yet another depth to the musical genre, they continue to re-animate the music as the basis of innumerable *versions*' (2008: 224, orginal emphasis). 'In Reggae, these drum and bass rhythms have become signature "riddim" tracks on which the Dancehall music scene flows' (Henriques 2008: 12). There is a distinction within these statements that relate specifically to dub music and this is where the version and dub categorization lie.

The concept of reinvention is a common theme in Jamaican culture and carries over to dub in many ways. In both sides of dub culture, version and dub, this plays out. With the creation of the rhythm track for sale, the music was reinvented to use the existing material in a new way in the dance hall. With the dub, the music was repurposed to create a new sound and song. Sonjah Stanley Niaah (2018) states: 'Jamaica just takes stuff and reinvents them, and that, for me, is perhaps the greatest gift we have given to the world'. This reinvention in music begins with the introduction of recording technology to the island and the shifts that occurred using this technology.

Another important distinction is made between version and dub in a discussion of songs that are recreated in cover versions. Evan Ware (2015), in *Their Ways: Theorizing Reinterpretation in Popular Music*, distinguishes between cover songs in two ways. He uses the term isomorphic for cover versions that stay close to the original song and metamorphic for those that stray farther from the original.

> They are separate because the choice to remain faithful to the base song in a given passage is as much an interpretive decision, with its own meanings and implications, as it is to change the same passage. They are independent because between a choice to do something differently from the original there will always be some element that remains similar.
>
> (Ware 2015: 13)

These qualities are evident within Jamaican popular music when discussing version and dub. The version is more isomorphic, while the dub is metamorphic.

While Ware's discussion relates to distinct choices that are made when covering a song, the producer and engineer also make distinct choices on what elements to cut out, in the version, or what elements to change and modify, in the dub. The version, or foundation riddim, is often used to create a new variant over the original song by inserting a DJ or singer into the mix. The dub is a direct reconstruction of the already existing song, with choices made by the engineer and producer on what to remove and add. These choices are specific and become distinct elements of study.

For Henriques and others, the original musical track, particularly the bass line, is what creates and defines the riddim or 'foundation riddim'. Here, I am suggesting that this bass line is critical to the version track of dub music. Henriques also focuses on the sound system and dance-hall moments in his work brilliantly. The rhythm track or version is what DJs and sound systems used primarily to achieve connection and feel within the dance hall. The concept of manipulating these tracks to achieve a different sounding song for release and artistic creation takes on a different meaning.

Many others discuss riddim as the versioning of the same song and how this song has been dispersed throughout the world as a foundation of Jamaican music. These riddims are often manipulated and reused by different sound systems and DJs to insert their voice and feel into the song. This is where the version of the song takes precedence over the dub in dub music. The insertion of the DJ and voice does take place within a dub sometimes, but the majority of these versions rely on the original song structure with minimal changes in order to add vocals and call-outs.

An example of this would be the 'Answer' riddim. This song is structured on the bass line from the song 'I Will Never Let You Go' by Slim Smith. It is one of, what Michael Veal calls, the foundation riddims. There are countless versions of this rhythm that involve very few manipulations of the actual song except for the removal of the vocal tracks. This bass line has allowed many people to insert their vocals into the sound and has become famous throughout the world. This is a prime example of a version. The purpose of the reuse is for the DJ or sound system to insert themselves into the song.

To contrast this would be the dub where the engineer inserts themselves and makes extreme changes to the original track. A mix by King Tubby of Augustus Pablo such as 'King Tubby Meets Rockers Uptown' is a key example here. The song was a hit originally but became a huge hit after King Tubby manipulated the song and made it his own. The distillation of sound also plays a large role here in the determination between version and dub.

The distinction between version and dub revolves around the discussion on commodity culture and the ways in which an artifact of culture becomes a commodity or resists it. This distinction plays out in dub culture with these two genres, both of which are attempts to gain money for the producer. When listening to these different artifacts, the manipulation and work within the track stand out. The more manipulation that occurs, the more resistant to becoming a commodity the artifact becomes. While both version and dub are essentially commodities, the dub seeks to propel the engineer and producer to the forefront of the track. The version still seeks to maintain the original musicianship and song structure.

The original, always a part of the track in dub culture, becomes a referent point for the audience. The difference between a dub and a version is the amount of manipulation that occurs. In a version, the audience is completely aware of the original song as the version uses the original melody to establish the track. In a dub, this does not have to occur. It does occur, occasionally, depending on the producer and engineer, but the differences are the key. In a version, the audience is given manipulations of a fader on the mixing board and certain frequency shifts in EQ and sometimes vocal insertions, whereas with a dub, the engineer is prominent in their insertions.

Through the limited production of the dubplate, and even limited runs of dub albums, the music of dub is a commodity of culture but one that resists many issues with consumer products. Both version and dub are produced for monetary gain. The difference lies in the amount of change that the producer and engineer create. These changes allow for the art of the engineer and producer to take precedence over the original track, creating a way for the audience to listen differently to the song. In both version and dub, these changes are heard. In the dub, the song is much more influenced by the engineer and their techniques of manipulation.

There is a further distinction that must be made as well. This is the term 'special', which is a one-off recording for a specific sound system. Specials were dubplates that were only made for use in a specific dance or sound system. The singer, vocalist, or DJ would call out the sound system and say they were the 'baddest sound in town' or some other hyperbolic shout-out, over a track that was already known. Many of these tracks were versions from previous recording sessions and were being reused strictly for the sound system. These specials, today, are usually called dubplates, and this is a confusing shift in language for many people.

The dubplate market was primarily centred around the dance halls and sound systems of the island. As the version track came into prominence, the DJs began using it as a way to insert their voice into the dance hall. An example of a more contemporary sound system that is based off of the original model would be Stone Love in Jamaica. Tony Meyers (2018), sound system builder and owner of Jam 1, states: 'Stone Love demonstrated and showed that sound system is a business and not just playing out. I had the privilege to meet King Jammy and Black Scorpio and all of them teach me'. This business mindset also led to the development of specials, which were versions of songs specifically for certain sound systems or DJs.

Specials are specific vocal insertions that celebrate a sound system, DJ or anything that the producer would like to celebrate. These specials originally would only be recorded and released as a dubplate for a specific dance or celebration. Many DJs would only record a special with a date and time mentioned in it so that the producer could not reuse the recording again. Specials are still being made throughout the world today with original and contemporary DJs being paid to mention a sound system or club.

Augustus 'Guisse' Clarke, O.D. (2018) discussed the importance of his studio in cutting dubplates and specials for the sound systems.

> All the major record producers, the Channel Ones, Lee 'Scratch' Perry, all of dem came and gave us their tapes to say cut dubs for all the sound systems. I swapped a tube amplifier with Errol Dunkley for a cut of a rhythm called 'Baby I Love You' and then I had U Roy do a song on it, 'The Higher the Mountain'.
>
> (Clarke, O.D. 2018)[3]

Version and Dub

The use of the rhythm by the DJs is another distinguishing factor between version and dub. If the track was manipulated too much by the engineer or producer, the DJ would not have the room to voice anything over the manipulations. The ways in which the cultural language shifts as dub is carried throughout the world are also important.

When dub music appears in England for the first time, it is the dub that is played on the radio and what is distilled. This is discussed later in this book but is important here because the naming of dub shifts when it arrives in England. What the engineer did to the music starts to become much more prevalent in England and the engineers begin to get more and more credit. Katz (2019) states:

> When dub gets to England, it took on a life of its own because it didn't have the same connotation and purpose. In Jamaica, everything was based around a 45, while in England it was based around a full-length album.
>
> (n.pag.)

To set up a distinction here, you can look at the reception of Prince Buster's version album *The Message Dubwise* and King Tubby's *King Tubbys Meets Rockers Uptown*.

Both of these albums are fully discussed later in this book, but for this moment Prince Buster's album is an example of a version while King Tubby's is a dub. The producer is the highlight of Buster's while the engineer takes precedence in Tubby's. Both records were hits in England and began the distribution and distillation of Jamaican music throughout the world.

The removal or separation of the vocal track that occurred after the recording was complete is the beginning of the dub and is the version. What happens after that, and is done by the engineer, becomes the dub. As the music was brought around the world, certain songs became foundation riddims and helped to disperse and distill the sound of Jamaica. Now when people say riddim, they mean these foundations riddims and re-productions that are based on these original songs. It is meaningful in this discussion that some people do not know where most of these foundation riddims came from originally. People in the contemporary world may know what the 'Answer' riddim is and sounds like, but not the source track where it began. They may know what the 'Stalag' riddim is as well but not the original musicians and singers on the track.

The same, unfortunately, goes for the engineers that were a part of the creation of these original dubs. People are aware of the leading names in dub, but because of the speed of recording and pressing, producers were often given credit for the work of the musicians and engineers. When the music becomes dub this switches, and the engineers begin to gain the credit they deserve. There is still debate over who did what in what studio but through research, one can find out who engineered certain songs and full-length records.

How rhythm influences a culture is paramount to this discussion as well. Both version and dub rely on the song and musicians to provide a recording that relates to people and influences the surrounding culture. These musicians were highly trained, in most cases, and originally performed live for hotel and club audiences throughout the island. It is extremely interesting to discover the differences between playing styles in the uptown tourist hotels and clubs and the downtown dance halls, but that is for another time. The playing styles of these musicians informed and created what dub would become. Groups like the Skatalites, Byron Lee & the Dragonaires, and many others founded what became known as Jamaican music. Dub begins with these musicians playing ska, rocksteady and reggae first in order for the rhythm to be developed.

It is not just the end result that is important to dub; it is how the music got recorded to the track that made the original sound of dub. This has changed in the contemporary world and is an important discussion to be had as well. The engineers who understand the importance of who is playing what type of instrument were the key to the original music. Guisse Clarke, O.D. (2019) states:

> It is the engineer that knew who has this bass guitar, what equipment gives me this sound, how do I try to create a unique sound, that formed dub. In the old days, it took time to mix and focus on the sound, now it is not so much about sound, but getting something quickly.
>
> (n.pag.)

Cunningham (2019) discussed the meaning of dub as well and linked it to gospel and the feeling of church music. Finding dub she stated:

> It completely consumed me and to me, music is a spiritual thing. Instrumental dub is responsible for the Jah 9 that you all know today. As a poet from an early age, I went into the space that became Dub Club on skyline drive, I felt moved and felt space in the music that I could create in. It was a healing for me.
> (Cunningham 2019)

This connection allowed her to create in a different way and shifted her focus into what her music has become today. The issue of taking time and working within the sound of the music is the point for her as well.

The speed of creation and the ways that dub has changed through its distillation frame this book. The ways in which version and dub go in and out of the conversation of reggae also become important to this music. The terminology of rhythm to version to dub to foundation riddim all form dub music and have distilled the sound of Jamaica throughout the world. You can dub anything and expose any type of music to a dub process, but what dub is and what it has become today is the focus of this conversation and how, through the music of dub, we can distinguish a culture and framework for existence.

Chapter 2
Java, Java, Java, Java and *Aquarius Dub*: The Start of a Culture

Figure 2.1: Original pressing of *Java, Java, Java, Java*. Photo by Cassandra Abbey (2020).

The claim of what the first dub record was is contentious and filled with rumors. For many, and for the purpose of this work, *Java, Java, Java, Java* (1973), released by Clive Chin and performed by the Impact All Stars, and *Aquarius Dub* (1973), produced and mixed by Herman Chin-Loy and engineered by Carlton Lee, are the beginning. Both are instrumental works that focus on how the track of music can be manipulated, and these records demonstrate the first manipulations that would go on to become representative of dub music and sound. The mixes feature the bass line and situate the rhythm within the lower register of sound. The drums and other instruments come in and out throughout each track, and there are consistent sweeps of the cymbal created with the high-pass filter on the mixing board. The change of the stereo sound through panning of various instruments is throughout the tracks. This panning creates a swirling sound on each song and allows the music to feel larger than the raw track. Dub music features these sounds, and many became signature techniques for different engineers.

These two records can also be codified as version records in the dub genre. The songs here focus more on the reuse and re-imaging of hit songs and less on the manipulation of the track. There are manipulations, discussed below, but the intent of these two records was to profit financially off the existing tracks by using them in a different way. As stated previously, the music of dub was always about making money for the producers, but these two records demonstrate how tracks were re-used and re-published in a different way without as much influence from the engineer as later dub works would represent. The end of this remixing, for these records, was to extend the sounds and tracks as commodities. These were producer records and the beginnings of a development in sound. Michael Veal (2007), in *Soundscapes and Shattered Songs in Jamaican Reggae* states:

> What made dub unique in the context of pop music both in Jamaica and worldwide was the creative and unconventional use recording engineers made of their equipment (as, for example, in using acetate as the dubplate). This enabled them to fashion a new musical language that relied as much on texture, timbre, and soundspace, as it did on the traditional musical parameters of pitch, melody, and rhythm.
>
> (64)

The creation of these soundspaces was the point of dub and was the difference between dub and other forms of Jamaican popular music. The performance of the music was key but had already been heard before. Now, the version and dub were for the audience to hear what had been done to the song to create a soundspace. Veal's discussion on texture and timbre falls into this process of creation and establishes the main difference between dub and other forms of music from Jamaica.

Java, Java, Java, Java, recorded in 1972 and released in 1973, comes in as one of the first dub records to be released and features the Impact All Stars who included Earl 'Chinna' Smith (guitar), Fully Fullwood (bass), Augustus Pablo (keys and melodica), Winston Wright (keyboard), Tommy McCook (Saxophone) and others. Clive Chin produced the record, and the engineer was Errol Thompson. The recording took place at Studio 17 above Randy's records in Kingston. The manipulation of the track is not as deliberate as on *Aquarius Dub*, but the removal and insertion of different instruments in each track laid the foundation for dub music. David Katz (2012) discusses the album in *Solid Foundation: An Oral History of Reggae*,

> 'Java, Java, Java, Java' was one of the first dub albums, issued in a limited pressing of 1,000 copies in 1973. Thompson keeps the bass at the top of the mix for the whole disc, shuffling in reverb-treated keyboards, guitar, horns, and the odd snatch of vocals or melodica.
> (186)

The track 'Java Dub' features Augustus Pablo on melodica and became a huge breakthrough hit. This was one of the first re-productions of a hit song into the dub format. By taking existing songs that were already hits and remixing them, Thompson and Chin allowed for the addition of Pablo and other musicians to the track. Dub music was born from this idea to reuse and repurpose the existing tracks and *Java, Java, Java, Java* does just that. The tracklist is A1 'Guiding Dub', A2 'Cheating Dub', A3 'E.T. Special', A4 'Soulful Dub', A5 'Ordinary Version Dub', B1 'Java Dub', B2 'Meet Me Dub', B3 'Black Man's Dub', B4 'King Babylon Dub' and B5 'Hide Away Dub'. Each track demonstrates the elements that form the culture of dub and display powerful moments in the beginnings of this culture.

Social 1

In 1972, Jamaica experienced a shift in political ideology. From 1972 to 1983, the country went through a political battle between the People's National Party (PNP) that, in 1974, declared Democratic Socialism as the new political framework in Jamaica and the Jamaican Labour Party (JLP) who claimed Social Democracy. In 1972, the Parliament dissolved, and general elections saw the PNP gain control of the government with Michael Manley in control of the country. This shift changed, both positively and negatively, the way people viewed the government. The major shift with this change was in the attention that the government gained from the populace. Post-independence was one of the more contentious and discussed periods in Jamaica. A *New York Times* article by Stephen Davis (1976) states: 'Kingston is a city of fires, a city on fire, and whether the flames will be contained is the question Jamaicans are asking themselves' (153). The music reflected and influenced many of these cultural changes and attitudes.

The battle between the parties branched out into the streets and created a culture in Kingston that was very different from the resorts on the north shore. The Manley-led PNP was often accused of Communism and often linked to Cuba, while the JLP was the conservative side of the argument and wanted strict reform. Rumor of political-led gangs interfering with government rallies and meetings ran wild and the people were split along financial lines as well. Manley supported the lower classes, particularly Rastafarianism through his invitation to Emperor Haile Selassie I. A Jamaican reporter (1976) in the same *New York Times* article states:

> 'When Manley came to power, Jamaica was given one of those rare last chances a country sometimes gets. At the time we were little more than another banana republic with a squalid right-wing oligarchy ruling us. Now one hears so much about Communism and selling out to Cuba, but if the Socialist programs are allowed to mature, we'll have the chance to become an austere but free and outspoken society of the left'.
>
> (cited in Davis 1976: 153)

The concept of a 'free and outspoken society of the left' is one that continues to be held and argued for in contemporary times.

In 1973, the government developed a minimum wage for workers and also announced that all secondary schools would be free in Jamaica and that Jamaicans could attend the University of the West Indies tuition free. This led to a large increase in attendance and by 1974 educational reform. The society was changing, and the classes were developing a voice. The lower class, downtown, voice that had been somewhat quiet gained prominence.

The JLP and others kept undermining these programs based on the money needed to put them into place. This added to the separation between social classes that are still relevant today. The music of the north shore resorts and uptown Jamaica was still the bright ska, calypso and mento often stereotyped as 'Island Music', while the music of the street went darker.

Dub music captures this darker tone of the society, but the producers focused originally on the reuse of the existing track to gain more money. In 1973, an oil crisis struck Jamaica that left the country with financial difficulties it is still dealing with. This crisis also framed the feeling of the country as it shifted culturally. The divide between social classes deepened and the separation between uptown and downtown expanded. Through this separation, the producers began to look for new ways to capitalise on the existing music that they had on hand. This reuse is a significant feature of Jamaican society and, during this time, music began to become a part of it.

Previously, Jamaican popular music centered on r&b and other forms of American music. This sound was played at house parties and street dances by the sound systems. Owners like Duke Reid and Clement 'Sir Coxsone' Seymour Dodd would spin American records for these parties in order to sell liquor and to advertise their stores. The most popular sound systems were Arthur Duke Reid's 'The Trojan' and Dodd's 'Sir Coxsone's the Downbeat'. Both predate dub and are the beginning of Jamaican popular music. When the 1970s hit, Jamaica was looking for a different sound.

This sound came from the ska and rocksteady that developed out of American r&b and soul music. *Java, Java, Java, Java* and *Aquarius Dub* reflect this sound on some tracks, but they are what occurred after ska and rocksteady had become popular. These records are the sound of the producers using ska and rocksteady to increase their income and to reuse the records in a different way. The deeper timbre of these tracks is heard in the levels of bass and through the removal of higher-toned instruments.

Clive Chin began working at Randy's Record Store selling records and then at the associated studio Randy's Studio 17 on 17

North Parade. Chin began Impact!, the record label, and needed a studio to record the label's releases. Chin (2003: n.pag.) stated:

> We wanted to establish our own label. So after my father had the Randy's label, from the early '60s pretty much up to the end of the '60s, my uncle, who is deceased now, had brought a recording job sheet back from New York that had the name Impact!, and I fell in love with that name instantly. I said, 'Uncle, can I just use this beautiful name?' And he says, 'Yes, sure, go for it.' The Impact! label was the flagship for all of my early recordings that took me through '70 to '79, when the studio was closed.

This need also led to the development of dub rhythms. For Chin, 'To put the whole thing in its right respective place, I say, a good music is a music that sells. It's a selling music, money music' (n.pag.).

The stories of a dubplate being produced for a specific dance and being played to the crowd who loved it are throughout the culture of dub and Jamaica. The DJs would play a record and watch the reaction from the crowd. If the crowd asked for the song and loved it, then the DJs and others would go back to Chin and other record labels and the song would be fully pressed for release. These dubplates were sometimes called pre-releases and often viewed as collectors' items.

This concept of a 'selling music' defines the split between version and dub. Chin is not at all hesitant to define good music as music that sells and the records that were produced for Impact! did sell. The process of reusing songs that sold in a different way allowed for Chin and others to make more money off the already recorded sounds. This was not the type of dub that would later become an artistic statement on its own, even though it does carry artistic qualities; this was dub for the strict purpose of making money and focusing on gain for the producer. *Java, Java, Java, Java* and *Aquarius Dub* may be the first full albums of dub, but they were relying on techniques and forms that had already been established and using songs that already had demand.

Timbre 1

Timbre is oftentimes subjective in other forms of music but with dub, the timbre must focus on the lower end of the auditory

Java, Java, Java, Java and *Aquarius Dub*

Figure 2.2: Bookshelf of reel-to-reel tape at Anchor studios. Photo by Author.

spectrum. This lower-end resonates and creates sensations in the body that allows dub music to connect to the person in ways that differ from other forms of music. *Java, Java, Java, Java* and *Aquarius Dub* achieve this timbre in similar ways. Through the removal of the higher-end instruments, such as guitar and piano in places in the song and through an equalizing technique using

23

a high-pass filter, this low-end timbre appeared prominently on record for the first time. Ray Hitchins (2014) in *Vibe Merchants: The Sound Creators of Jamaican Popular Music* states:

> The sound of emphasized bass therefore provides an opportunity to assess how the audio engineer acts as a sonic mediator between the sound system and recording studio, influencing not only the recording process but also the way in which music is created, captured and consumed.
>
> (80)

The first two tracks on *Java, Java, Java, Java* demonstrate this bass end timbre.

The engineer as a 'sonic mediator' is what dub is all about. The focus on deeper tones and the importance of the bass resonating through the sound system was paramount in the development of dub. The engineers became known for getting the loudest, roundest, deepest, bass on the record. Thompson and Morris were the key engineers in these original moments.

Errol Thompson, known as ET, began as an engineer under Sylvan Morris at Studio One. His first song was Max Romeo's 'Wet Dream' before he went to Randy's. His style of mixing and experimentation was the foundation for dub music. Harry Hawks (2013) for the website Reggae Collector states: 'Errol's engineering innovations began to shape and form the early stirrings of dub and the switches on the Studio 17 board, as opposed to King Tubby's faders, gave his music a unique and totally individual sound' (n.pag.). This individual sound was developed through the soundscape and vibe that were created in the studio by Thompson with Chin's production.

After some time, Thompson got together with Joe Gibbs and they became known as 'the Mighty Two'. Their recordings were pivotal in establishing Jamaican music throughout the world and led to the breakthrough of many artists Hawks stated:

> If I could turn back the hands of time Errol would never leave Randy's. He was the innovative one. I felt like something left me when he left [...] an innovative producer. You see Errol is the history of certain music in the seventies.
>
> (2013: n.pag.)

'Guiding Dub', A1, is one of the earliest examples of manipulating a track in these ways and has some early specifications added to it that would later be used or removed by other engineers and producers. The easiest one to witness here is by leaving the main vocal line for the first verse and a bit of the hook; the audience has a referent to the original song. After establishing the song, the vocals are removed, and the trombone and bass carry the track forward. The guitar plays a stick lead part that matches the bass line and adds to the heaviness of the track. The piano and chorded guitar play on the upbeats throughout the original track, but in this version, they are removed and added in sporadically to allow for the bass tone to carry the song.

This also occurs in the next track A2 'Cheating Dub'. After the intro, the vocal track starts the song so that the audience is set up for the dub version. The difference with this track is that the tempo is faster, and the vocals are used a bit more to remind us of the original track. You can even hear the bleed over of the vocals onto the drum track if you listen carefully. Even at the slightly faster tempo, the track still retains its heavy tone by focusing on the way that the bass line interacts with the drums. In this song, the hi-hat is mixed very loudly, compared to the other tracks on the record, and the sound almost forces the listener to hear how the bass line works in between the hits on the hi-hat.

The bass line in this track blends with the high hat to create a drive and flow that had not been fixated on before. The bass line moves through the chord changes as the hi-hat hits play a steady pattern propelling the groove of the song. As this occurs, the piano and guitar are brought in and out of the song to keep the referent in place.

Rhythmic interplay 1

Rhythmic interplay is the way that the higher-end instruments accentuate the pulse of the track and help the grounded bass timbre propel through the mix. With rhythmic interplay, the main difference in Jamaican music is that the upbeat is stressed in the guitar and piano. This allows for the guitar to accent the bass and drum line as opposed to other musical forms that act in the opposite way. While doing so, the guitar and piano form another rhythm instrument instead of leading the way in the song. This rhythmic interplay comes from the upbeat and is the distinct difference between ska, reggae, dub and other forms of music. This is the Jamaican sound, to accent the upbeat with the higher-end guitars and pianos and to focus on the bass and drums as the lead. Especially with dub, the bass and drums take on even more prominence as the higher-end rhythmic interplay is often removed from the mix completely or added into the mix sporadically.

'E.T. Special', A3, the third track on *Java, Java, Java, Java*, demonstrates this upbeat pattern of the guitar and allows the guitar to propel the track while the bass line rides between the upbeats. It is not the 1, 2, 3, 4 beat pattern of rock music; the guitar hits on the 'and' of the beat so it is 1 and, 2 and, 3 and, 4 and. One listen to 'E.T. Special' will allow you to hear the guitar rhythmic interplay throughout the track. It is interesting that this track has the guitar consistently throughout the mix. It is not removed in places, as is often the case in dub, and therefore the track is a good example of the rhythmic interplay that is important to dub. The guitar pattern here is also a straight upbeat with the guitar only hitting one chord an offbeat.

'E.T. Special' was one of the songs on this album that sold well. The track features Tommy McCook on tenor sax and represents a connection to the Skatalites and others from Alpha Boys School. The focus on the tenor saxophone solo may be the reason that this track keeps the guitar rhythmic interplay throughout the whole song. This rhythmic interplay allows for the song to also be framed by the horn line and follow a standard jazz structure of head-solo-head.

The next track on the album represents this type of rhythmic interplay as well but has the guitar playing more than one stroke per upbeat. This pattern is another version of Jamaican rhythmic interplay that was often utilised in ska but became very popular in the reggae and dub style. The sound of this guitar rhythmic interplay is a chucka sound that is created by playing an upstroke and downstroke still on the 'and' of the beat. In 'Soulful Dub', A4, the guitar does this throughout the original song and is added and removed in places throughout the dub version. The higher end is dominant at the beginning of the song to introduce it and to make it recognisable to the audience and then it is removed to allow the drums and bass to carry the next section. The rhythmic interplay returns with the piano and guitar adding to the pulse and then they are removed again. This consistent back and forth of higher and lower end timbre suggests what will become of dub in the following years. There is also auxiliary percussion in this song that is barely audible, and this carried on throughout dub culture.

Re-production 1

The re-production of a song of dub becomes extremely important in each of the engineer's style and fluctuation of the track. In looking at how a song is constructed, we can differentiate from the producers and engineers who developed their own ways of creating and manipulating it. The ways in which the higher end is removed and placed in the track is just the beginning of the forms of re-production that were used. The insertion of sounds and the grounding of a track with auxiliary percussion and other natural elements also played a role in the re-production of the dub. In the early albums of dub, the main use of the re-production was the manipulation of the track and levels of the instruments. There were also uses of high-pass filters and other forms of delay and reverb, but the main manipulation of the track was in the removing and adding of the instruments.

Another form of addition and manipulation would later go on to influence music around the world, and this was the addition of the toaster or MC who would sing or talk over the track of music in the dance hall. One of the main reasons for dub's popularity was these toasters and MCs making a traditional song their own. This was not often recorded but is represented on *Java, Java, Java, Java* in 'Ordinary Version Dub', A5.

On 'Ordinary Version Dub', the track starts in one musical key with the guitar stick lead following the bass line. Then the vocal track comes in, which is Errol Thompson as the engineer and Eric 'Biggy Bunny' Lamont as the student. The music stops by stating 'hold up, wait a minute hold up then'. The engineer states, 'see here is the bass button' to the student and tells him to 'forward the bass'. At this point, the guitar stick lead enters in a different key and the track continues with the toaster whistling over the track. The track carries forward and just when the groove is established the engineer comes in again and stops the music. 'Hold on, hold on, just a likkle ['little']'. Thompson then tells the people to listen to the bass, then listen to the drum, then listen to the guitar and then listen to everything. The track literally builds the song for the listener.

You do not ever get into the full groove during this track, but the constructive element of dub is demonstrated completely here.

This building of a track from the engineer's point of view was not heard before this and has rarely been heard since on a track of music. It is extremely important in the development of Jamaican music from version to dub and signifies a shift to the importance of the engineer in the music. As Thompson 'shows us how to operate', the engineer takes over the track.

The next track on the album also demonstrates forms of re-production, or better yet destruction, in the way that the sounds are removed from the track to let the bass completely resonate. On 'Java Dub', B1, the track begins with a guitar line and a keyboard added on top of the mix. Then a melodica line comes in before everything, but the bass and drums are removed. The bass becomes the main melody line for the remainder of the track. The drums are placed very far back in the mix, except for the kick drum, and the guitar comes in and out of the mix throughout. 'Java Dub' represents the way that the fader moves in dub can be heard in a mix. As the track continues, elements come in and out to push the track as the bass remains on top and solidifies the melody.

The melodica line, played by Augustus Pablo over the beginning of the track, propelled this song into the charts. A simple line repeated twice and never heard again highlighted Pablo and started the use of the instrument as a main element of dub. 'Java Dub' created a path for Pablo to perform with the melodica and this carried through to many other recordings.

'Meet Me Dub', B2, takes a classic rocksteady song 'Meet Me at the Corner', originally sung by Dennis Brown, and re-constructs it focusing on the bass line as well. The song begins with the vocal line, like in 'Guiding Dub', but then removes everything aside from the bass and drums. The guitar comes in sporadically throughout the track but, again, the bass rides on top of the mix. As in the discussion on timbre, this creates a track that is full of space but one that resonates through the body.

The difference between the original song and the dub version here represents the ways in which dub can shape the soundscape and tone of a song to become darker and more ominous. The groove of the song is the point on this track, and the drums and bass make the track flow. The guitar and piano come in and out, but the track is completely deconstructed down to the bass line.

The next track on the album is 'Black Man's Dub', B3. This track is very interesting in terms of re-production as it focuses on the keyboard line but distorts it with a delay. The track would fit into the rhythmic interplay section, but this rhythmic interplay is thrown off by warping the track through effects. The bass line is still high in the mix, but the entire track sounds warped, and the keyboard line is almost out of time. The tuning and fluctuating of the elements in the track change as the different instruments come in. The only consistency here is in the drums and bass. 'Black Man's Dub' is one of the more interesting songs on this album in terms of re-production and creates a spacey sound throughout the track.

The organ being warped in this track is something that engineers have attempted to get on recording since this track was released. The sound is similar to the organ being played under water and the sound wave of the track shakes and warbles. This was achieved with the use of the Leslie speaker but through techniques developed by Thompson and carried forward to many other dub engineers and producers today.

Completion 1

The final two tracks on *Java, Java, Java, Java* bring all these elements into focus and create a closing to one of the first dub records to be produced. 'King Babylon Dub', B4, and 'Hide Away Dub', B5, share elements of timbre, rhythmic interplay and re-production that propel the music into the culture of dub. 'King Babylon Dub' begins with the main melody line and the guitar chucka chucka that represents the rhythmic interplay of dub and Jamaican music. Then, just as quickly, as it is in the track, the guitar disappears, and the bass line takes the lead. This bass line is the most complex of the album and sets the melody with the drums. The timbre is demonstrated here with a focus on the bass and the kick drum thumping throughout the track. The elements of re-production are not as complex as in previous tracks, but the removal and insertion of the guitar represent this element consistently with the other tracks on the record. The bass line carries the remainder of the song as the bass and drums are faded out to close the track.

In 'Hide Away Dub', you hear a similar structure. The main melody and rhythmic interplay in the guitar and piano begin the song and are then removed quickly to leave the bass carrying the melody and rhythm. There is more re-production here, as the guitar and piano come back in throughout the track, but the bass is on top keeping the timbre of the entire album. Other elements of re-production come through in the bass track itself. During the key change, the bass is warped and almost becomes out of time. The main melody line does not come back into the track, but the rhythmic interplay floats in and out and allows the timbre and re-production to resolve the album.

Social 2

The second record that began the culture of dub was *Aquarius Dub*, which was recorded at Aquarius Records, owned by Herman Chin-Loy's brother Lloyd and opened in 1969. The store was the first to bring in a 24-track mixing board, and this began the recording studio where many of the original dub and rocksteady tracks were recorded. Alton Ellis, Dennis Brown and Bruce Ruffin recorded there, reaching the charts in the United Kingdom in the early 1970s. The session band at Aquarius mostly was Lloyd Charmer's the Now Generation, which performed on many tracks with different singers. Charmer's approach to rocksteady was to focus on the arrangements and because of him, the music became more sophisticated in sound and structure. All of this created the perfect mixture to be dubbed and *Aquarius Dub* was formed.

The musicians on the record were Augustus Pablo (keys), Ansell Collins (keys), Michael 'Boo' Richards (drums), Geoffrey Chung (guitar and keys), Val Douglas (bass), Earl 'Wire' Lindo (keys and guitar), Mikey Chung (guitar and keys) and Robbie Lynn (keys). Each track on the record contains slightly different elements of dub, but the general focus on the bass and the deeper tones carries throughout the entire album. The bass is set highest in the mix, and the tone of the bass resonates throughout each track. The drums are also mixed extremely high throughout the record but come in and out differently per each track. The way that Chin-Loy manipulated the faders of the mixing board becomes the focus when listening to the individual songs. Where and what is removed from the mix and what is added to each track becomes the focus upon listening to the entire album. The tracklist is A1 'Jah Rock', A2 'Rumbo Malt', A3 'I Man', A4 'Oily', A5 'Rest Yourself', B1

'Jumping Jack', B2 'Heavy Duty', B3 'Jah Jah Dub', B4 'Nyah Time' and B5 'Jungle Rock'. This is set up as one of the first dub albums because of these differences between the tracks and the ways that the entire record plays with the changes.

This record also falls into the category of version dub as the focus was on the reuse of the songs to profit off already successful songs. At points on this record, the manipulations are very slight and differ from the original track minimally. Herman Chin-Loy was the first to bring a 24-track mixing board to Jamaica. His half-brother Lloyd Chin-Loy opened and ran the record store Aquarius Records in Half Way Tree, Kingston. From here, the studio began when Herman took to producing. Again, this is an example of tracks that were popular, being reused to expand the monetary gain. The version genre of dub would go onto influence the entire genre and *Aquarius Dub* was no different from *Java, Java, Java, Java*.

Both albums represent the ways in which music can become art and commodity. Jacques Attali (1985) states the function of music in three parts,

> it seems that music is used and produced in the ritual in an attempt to make people forget the general violence; in another, it is employed to make people believe in the harmony of the world, that there is order in exchange and legitimacy in commercial power; and finally, there is one in which it serves to silence, by mass-producing a deafening, syncretic kind of music, and censoring all other human noises.
>
> (19)

By reusing the existing tracks, these records can be codified as a version in the dub genre and also as the second part of Attali's definition of music.

Dub was also used to make people 'forget the general violence' of their surroundings as well, but many people would claim that dub is about making people believe in the harmony of the world through sound. By creating soundscapes that resonate with people, regardless of where they are from in the world, dub takes popular songs and recreates them for everyone. The harmony comes in the use of the bass and drums to focus the sound.

The third function here can be linked to pop music, and the version genre of dub could be classified as the pop music of

Jamaica. The suggestion here is that, because of the engineer's influence, these records were more linked to the statement that 'there is order in exchange and legitimacy in commercial power'. Loy and Chin's production of these albums does set them into the commodity realm and designates these records away from the artistic developments that would come later. They contain the first manipulations of the mixing board for this purpose.

Timbre 2

Herman Chin Loy produced *Aquarius Dub* and inserted his and Carlton Lee's sound into the developing culture. This album, for many, signified the beginning of dub music and forced the DJs and MCs to hear a newer sound with the focus being on the bass timbre. The first track 'Jah Rock', A1, begins with a slight guitar line and then fixates on the bass throughout. The song uses the stick lead of the guitar sporadically, but the focus is on the bass line. The drums are even removed in parts, and the swell of the cymbals is heard through a panning technique.

While the track swirls between the left and right speaker channel, the bass line drives the listener in a way that was not fixated on before. While the songs on *Java, Java, Java Java* do this, the opener of *Aquarius Dub* is much more bass heavy and uses the bass frequency as the main part of the song. The cymbal splash that occurs in the middle of the track would also resonate through dub culture and be heard many times again. The sound of the cymbal is smashed and not allowed to resonate, as in a typical mix. Then the sound is pushed, by Lee, from one speaker to the other side in the short resonance that is allowed. This smashing and panning of the cymbal created a warped sound that would influence many more engineers.

The second track on the album, 'Rumbo Malt', A2, begins with a fast ska line, and again the heavy bass tone is the focus. Here, the track quickly switches to a slower groove with the bass and drums driving the sound. The piano and guitar are mixed in occasionally to propel the track and then everything disappears aside from the drums. In this mix, you can hear the way that Lee mixed the drums. They do not have the standard high pitch resonance of drums, typical of rock music, as they sound muted and almost dull. This is due to the high-pass filter that was used on the entire track and what allows the timbre to be stabilised in the bass register. The entire track of 'Rumbo Malt' carries this tone and continues the fixation on the bass register.

These two opening tracks demonstrate many techniques and uses of effects that would carry through all of reggae and eventually get to all of popular music. The sound of the drums and the manipulation of the cymbals are key elements of dub that are featured in these tracks.

Rhythmic interplay 2

As in *Java, Java, Java, Java*, the guitar and piano lines of each track come in and out to propel and move each song. What is interesting about dub culture is where these elements are used in different ways and times to syncopate the song and to give the audience a specific referent point. In the third track of *Aquarius Dub*, 'I Man', A3, the rhythmic interplay leads the song and comes in at different places throughout it to give the listener something to latch onto. The track begins with the main melody line quickly being heard and then it drops out to give way to the bass. The drums have a shuffle pattern here in the high hat that also propels the rhythm, but the main interest is where the rhythmic interplay of the piano and guitar comes in and where it is removed. The upstroke of the guitar and piano starts the track and then is heard in various parts of the song. This rhythmic interplay plays with the drum and bass pattern until everything is cut out. There is a resonance of the track that can be heard, but the focus becomes the drums, followed by the bass line, and then the rhythmic interplay.

The drums are the focus of this song, which differentiates it from the others on the record and leads to a more syncopated feel. The pattern is a standard one drop pattern that was used throughout rocksteady. As the song carries forward, the drums take on a more dominant role and the other elements are mixed around them to give the track a lighter feel than the first two tracks on the album. Although the drums are still mixed with a dulling effect, possibly compression, which keeps the timbre of the track in line with the others, the rhythmic interplay is the key to 'I Man'.

'Oily', A4, is a much faster song that also demonstrates the rhythmic interplay used throughout dub and reggae. This track is mixed much brighter than the others are and carries the piano skank during most of the song. The bass and drums still lead the way, but the guitar stick lead and the piano skank are much more prominent, giving the track a lively feel that pushes the faster rhythm through the song. The song is recognisable to the audience and is not manipulated as much as the previous tracks, but the adding and removing of the guitar and piano are where the rhythmic interplay lies. There is a slight conga track in the mix as well, which adds to the rhythmic interplay in the drums. 'Oily' is one representation of how brighter songs were still used and mixed for dub. As the timbre of the bass and drums is still the focus, the melody in the guitar line and the skank in the piano are used here in a different way that highlights the melody. There is even a short guitar solo, or melody line, that comes in at the end of the track as it fades out.

Re-production 2

The first side of the album ends with a dub of Dennis Brown's version of Carole King's 'It's Too Late' entitled 'Rest Your Self', A5. The Brown song was already a hit following the success of King's and the dub is an excellent example of re-production techniques that were used throughout dub. The track removes all of the drums in the beginning and leaves the skank of the guitar, the bass and stick lead lines, and Brown's vocals in. The entire vocal track is left here and is the focus of the song, but the way that the music is stripped out of the mix is the element of re-production. Even the sax solo only has the barest amount of music behind it. The bass line comes in and out of this track, while the drums are completely removed, and Brown's voice is the main focus.

On 'Rest Your Self', Brown's vocals are manipulated with a reverb and delay that makes them sound as if they are in a different space than the original. Although the track's speed is the same as the original, it sounds slower as the drums are removed, and the vocal and bassline dominate the sound. The mixing of the bass line is what becomes interesting throughout this track. How Lee brought the bass in and out of the vocal pattern makes this version fully constructed. While the alto sax line is high pitched and seems to come out of nowhere, it separates the chorus from the verse and also demonstrates the re-production of this track.

This track also demonstrates what producers would do to create a version for the sound system and dance hall. This song was known by everyone at the time and extremely popular in the original King song and cover by Brown. Here it gets treated by the engineer to re-sell the song. The focus is on what has been done to the song not on the song itself.

Side B opens with 'Jumping Jack', B1, which continues the example of Lee at the mixing board constructing the track. The organ is set way in the back of this track while the bass and drums carry the feel. The entire track is removed, aside from the bass line, and the original backing vocals can be heard in parts as bleed through from the recording. The drums are mixed heavy in tone again with the kick taking a dominant role here. The stick lead of the guitar blends with the bass line and the kick drum sits right between them. The element of the chords in the organ barely coming through is also an interesting constructive element that would continue to influence engineers in dub culture.

Then comes 'Heavy Dub', B2, which demonstrates the way in which Lee used a horn line within a dub track. The track begins with a small vocal saying 'heavy, heavy, heavy, heavy' with reverb and delay being used on it to introduce the track. There is an organ line, and the bass line dissolves into the main horn line of the song. This track is again a faster and more upbeat rhythm led by the horns, but then they are quickly removed to focus on the bass and stick lead of the guitar. The piano and organ remain very far removed in the background and then the entire track is bass. These fader moves are extremely important elements in the re-production of the dub track, and 'Heavy Dub' demonstrates these moves throughout the track with multiple musical elements. By removing everything except the bass line, the track moves only with the bass timbre and then everything comes back in towards the end. The horns act as a shell for the rhythm as they begin and end the track while the bass solidifies the melodic force.

'Jah Jah Dub', B3, also focuses on constructive elements. The song begins with an organ hit and then the bass and drums start the song. The organ then plays a melody line, and this melody line is what is removed and inserted throughout the driving bass and drums. Here, the drums are used in the re-production as they are removed and inserted as in 'Jumping Jack', but the organ hits and the timbre of the organ carry this dub. By doing so, 'Jah Jah Dub' differentiates itself from the rest of the tracks on the album. Much like 'Jumping Jack' in its use of the horns, this song fixates on the organ line and allows the bass line to flow under the melody. The bass still carries its own melody and is prominent in the mix, especially when the drums are removed, but the organ line is the focus here.

Completion 2
The last two tracks, much like *Java, Java, Java, Java*, demonstrate multiple elements of dub culture. 'Nyah Time', B4, begins with a harsh hitting of chords that have been constructed to sound distorted. Then the timbre of the bass washes over the entire track. The drums are compressed almost to complete distortion and the stick lead of the guitar is warped almost out of tune. The piano skank is heard in the background in places, which allows for the rhythmic interplay in the track, but the re-production of the fader moves and the way that the entire track is mixed focuses on the bass line. The other musical elements are distorted and, in some places, to the point of being out of key.

The album ends with 'Jungle Rock', B5. A more upbeat track that shares mixing elements with 'Nyah Time' in that the drums are distorted and the elements that are used come in as the bass line propels the track. The organ holds of the original song are heard but set back far in the mix, and the timbre of the song resonates in the bass frequencies. The main melody of the track is in the bass, and the drums propel it to end the album.

The end of the beginning
Java, Java, Java, Java and *Aquarius Dub* demonstrate the start of the culture of dub. With timbre, rhythmic interplay and re-production, these albums are the first lobbies into the sound of what dub would become. While these elements are not as drastically used here as in other albums that would soon be produced, they begin the discussion on how the engineer and producer frame the sound of dub. Don Ihde (2007) comments in *Listening and Voice: Phenomenologies of Sound*:

> The production of the recorded music lies behind and is presupposed by the end result. The studio is a complex location and process here involved. Acoustical space is constructed; takes, retakes, and increased musical editing goes into the development of the record such that a simple live-performance recording becomes but one possibility out of many.
>
> (261)

By shifting the timbre of the track to the bass frequencies, using the rhythmic interplay of the piano and guitar to insert melody, and constructing the track with fader moves, effects and other manipulations, Errol Thompson, Clive Chin and Herman Chin Loy produced the first efforts into dub and the culture that was formed around it. These two albums were not the first to utilise rhythm tracks, as other MCs and sound systems were already using the standard rhythm, but they were the first full-length releases to demonstrate the elements that created the culture of dub.

While the sound systems were catering to the live audience, the engineers and producers of dub were creating different sounds within already existing tracks. This was not a focus on who was chatting over what riddim; this was who was doing what to the musical elements of the song. In *Dub in Babylon: Understanding the Evolution and Significance of Dub Reggae in Jamaica and Britain from King Tubby to Post-Punk*, Christopher Partridge (2010) states:

> However, the point here is that, to quote Simon Reynolds, '[W]hat all the strands of dub theory share is the exaltation of producers and engineers over singers and players, and the idea that the studio effects and processing are more crucial than the original vocal or instrumental performances' (2000: 36).
>
> (60)

Dub culture was created based on these two albums and the elements that were used to create them. There was a live element to dub tracks, as they were distributed to the sound systems, but the sound of the track was the key to its success. What elements were removed and added became points of discussion for audience members and listeners and the culture of dub began to grow.

Chapter 3
Blackboard Jungle Dub and the Splicing of Culture

> Technology is taking over the world. What you take you give. Technology goes to the top.
>
> Lee 'Scratch' Perry (2019)

Figure 3.1: Lee 'Scratch' Perry and the author. Photo: Courtesy of Cassandra Abbey (2019).

Many people associate dub music with the engineer and producer Lee 'Scratch' Perry. Perry produced Bob Marley and many others at their beginnings and is one of the great artists to have come from Jamaica. He continues to tour and perform today and brings dub and its culture, to the world. Perry was the first to insert certain distinct sounds into his mix that defined his presence in the song. These insertions highlighted the ways that engineers assert themselves into the track of music. In *Lee 'Scratch' Perry: Kiss Me Neck: The Scratch Story in Words, Pictures, and Records*, Jeremy Lee Collingwood (2010) states:

> His inspiration for the new approach came from walking past a Pocomania ('little mania') Church and hearing the people wail. 'And me catch the vibration of them people!! Them was a spirit and dem tune me spiritually. That's where the thing come from – caus them Poco people getting sweet!'. He described his beat thus: '[...]a slower beat. A way beat, like stepping in glue. Them hear a different bass, a rebel bass, coming at you like a sticking gun'.
>
> (20)

Before this, the DJ used their voice to add to the basic track and the engineer removed or modified the track through frequency shifts and deletions. Perry began adding sounds to the rhythm track by using the space left during these removals. *Blackboard Jungle Dub* is an example of the dub genre in reggae as it demonstrates the artistic and creative force of the engineer. This was not just for capitalist gain; it was the engineer's creation and artistic statement.

The 'reputation of the specialist' can be heard in each track of dub and is the point of this section of the reggae genre. Lee 'Scratch' Perry developed his reputation before creating dub records, but it is in the dub that you can hear Perry's actual artistic statement. His reputation as a producer had been established with multiple hit songs but his insertions and sound effects assert his own voice as an artist. There is no escape from the collision of culture and commodity in our late capitalist system, but the artist can still be witnessed through dub. While the track is still a part of commodity culture, it establishes the engineer and/or producer by asserting their presence into the track. The collision between the specialist's autonomy and the culture industry is transformed in the dub track to allow for the engineer to stand out. This is a distinct creation of the entire dub genre and one that has transferred into contemporary times.

When discussing commodity culture, the designation between producer and engineer is extremely important. With Perry, both functions cross over and his 'vision' for the track was the key. The idea of creation for the purpose of selling is in direct opposition to the idea of creation for the purpose of just creating. In this album, the artist as engineer and producer comes through. This is not to say that the idea of selling music was absent from Perry's viewpoint and his issues with musicians and artists being 'taken' from him suggest that he was extremely aware of the profitability of these artists. There is a difference in what Perry did in the studio from Thompson, Morris and even Tubby that cannot be codified.

The specific parts of each track of music can be defined as the atoms of the song. The suggestion here is that these atoms are the parts that have been manipulated by the engineer. They are also the insertions that are added through effects, samples and other electronic forms. The discussion of the atoms of music stems from Adorno and other theorists in the modern time and the intent here is to discuss these atoms as intricate parts of each song.

The atoms of dub music are the most important part for the engineer and are what brings the engineer to the point of relevance and importance. The atoms represent part of the spell that the totality has lost. In live performance, the spell is there, but the recording does something to the live-ness of the music. Therefore, the atoms of the piece take precedence. The different parts of the song begin to stand out, and the listener can fixate on these parts as they listen to the repetition in the dance hall or through performance. The specific movement of the music, the shifts within the song and the way the composer brings different elements to life all take precedence over the totality of the song with the repetition heard with the record.

The dub then becomes another occurrence of this repetition and a part of the culture surrounding the music of Jamaica. Songs heard from American radio were refashioned to create Jamaican music that eventually turned into ska. Ska then transferred into rocksteady, reggae and both genres of dub, version and dub, emerge through repetitive listening. This goes even further when placing the composition into the hands of the engineer and producer and allowing them to create something new. The specific movements then become reflections of the engineer and producer. This only could have occurred with the previous version productions, such as *Java, Java, Java, Java* and *Aquarius Dub*. The developments in technology that had occurred also led to these shifts.

The unique qualities of the track are what the engineer and producer are looking for. They use small fragments of the track to bring out something different. The intent is to produce a sound that is separate from the original track, but familiar to the audience. As the Modern classical composers did with their shifts in compositional style and form, the engineer and producer bring new significance to the music.

These are the atoms of dub. Tubby and Perry, through manipulation of the track, give the atoms of the music precedence. When the listener hears the music, they are hearing the specific sounds and atoms of music that have been brought out by the producer and engineer. Much like hearing Beethoven on the radio, where the audience begins to hear the shifts in form, dub allows the audience to hear the distinct shifts in a form that have been accomplished by technology.

This is where the dub genre in reggae takes place. *Blackboard Jungle Dub* represents a way that an engineer and producer formed a cultural commodity with artistic intent. The importance here is in the insertions done by the engineer and how these go against what was selling and popular at the time. Compared to *Java, Java, Java, Java* and *Aquarius Dub,* this record resists popular conceptions of what to do with the tracks. This was a different assertion by Perry. One that became popular, but not because of the original tracks and what was done to them, but because of Perry's insertions and manipulations. The record stands outside of a pure commodity in this way. It was an attempt to make money off the reuse of tracks, like the version genre, but here you heard examples of the engineer directly.

The mixing board then becomes the instrument for the dub engineer and the technical elements of reverb, delay and other effects become the dominant focus. In *America on Record: A History of Recorded Sound,* Andre Millard (2005) gives a brief but effective explanation of dub. 'A *dub* was the name for both the sound and the piece of the recording which was edited into it' (Millard 2005: 360). The insertion is the point here, and the ways that the recording is manipulated are the shift in technology.

Millard's definition of the different parts of dub is interesting as it separates the song from the sonic insertions done by the engineer. It is also important to reassert the difficulty in the language of what dub is, demonstrated here. To dub something is an act of the engineer or producer, a dub is the song itself with these insertions and fader moves, and a version is what the engineer did through the removal of the vocal track. All of these definitions could not have occurred without the technology involved.

The developments in mixing board technology and the reel-to-reel recorder allowed this to happen and created a shift throughout the musical world. In Jamaica, this development created a means to expand the use of recorded music. The version genre of Jamaican music became ways for the producers to use technology in a new way for monetary gain. This is the beginning of sampling and other forms of manipulation that still occur today. These producers and engineers were creating and shifting the ways that we hear music through the technology of the mixing board and reel-to-reel recorder.

David Toop (2008), in 'Replicant: On dub', furthers this discussion on the effective nature of replication and the creation of new spaces of identity. He fixates his work on how, through replication, there is something gained for the listener. 'The composition has been decomposed, already, by the technology' (Toop 2008: 355), and the decomposition allows for the resurgence of sound and identity to take place. The identity coincides with the dub section of reggae. The first albums discussed did not care to establish an identity of the engineer. Although the engineer's created the sounds and movements of each song, the producers were the focus. These were attempts at expanding the sales of the tracks that they had in possession already. With *Blackboard Jungle Dub* (1973), this becomes about the identity of the producer and engineer.

In the *Blackboard Jungle Dub* album, we can see the destructive nature of dub and the rebuilding of sound structures on top of the original music or form. The point is not to hear the song but what the engineer and producer have done 'to it'. The record opens with a call out to all the 'meek and humble' and begins a track of soundscape in which you can barely distinguish the original song. What you can hear, even on the very first listen, is that the sounds have been manipulated, destroyed, added to and reimagined. The first track, 'Blackboard Jungle Dub (version 1)', contains musical elements that move the listener through the track, but the focus remains on the elements that have been removed and how the track has been added to. The addition of delay on the flute creates an atmosphere of space, and the drums are placed in the extreme background of the mix. Erik Davis (2008), in '"Roots and Wires" remix', suggests: 'Dub's analog doppelgangers, spectral distortions, and vocal ghosts produced an imaginal space' (63). By making the snare drum sound like a machine gun in places the track sounds militaristic. This album was limited in production to only 300 copies and was not found outside of Jamaica very often until its recent re-release. David Katz (2000), in *People Funny Boy: The Genius of Lee 'Scratch' Perry*, suggests: 'Whatever the case, *Blackboard Jungle Dub* showed the very power of dub to transform a piece of music, to radically alter any given composition through creative mixing and spatial representation' (177).

The 'creative mixing' is the focal point of the dub genre and how it differentiates itself from the version genre discussed previously. Morris, Thompson and others were genius in their mixing and creative moments in the studio, but the focus was on the reuse of the original song, not on what they inserted into the track. I am making a very fine distinction here that is very difficult to write about as the sound must be heard to make this entirely clear. All of these engineers inserted their feelings and presence into the track in different ways.

This album, originally released as 'Upsetters 14 Dub' in 1973, was the seventh release from the Upsetters. The Upsetters were the house band for Black Ark studios and began with Gladstone Anderson on piano, Alva Lewis on guitar, Glen Adams on organ and the Barrett brothers, Aston 'Family Man' Barrett on bass and Carlton Barrett on drums. With this lineup, they recorded a good deal of tracks for Lee Perry with King Tubby at the controls of the mixing console. Their first release, entitled 'Return of Django', was successful in creating the genre and the double – A-side release 'Return of Django'/'Dollar in the Teeth' peaked at #5 on the UK singles chart in 1969. The Barrett brothers eventually joined Bob Marley and became part of the Wailers. After their departure, Perry found new musicians to take their roles and the Upsetters continued.

With the shift of musicians, Perry continued the Upsetters with Boris Gardiner on bass, Mikey Richards, Sly Dunbar and Benbow Creary on drums, Earl 'Chinna' Smith on guitar and Winston

Wright and Keith Sterling on keyboards. Both groups of musicians perform on *Blackboard Jungle Dub*, fully titled *Upsetters 14 – Dub Blackboard Jungle*, along with guest instrumentalists.

Although this group of musicians was responsible for the actual music on most, if not all, of Lee Perry's early recordings, the Upsetters were all schooled musicians that had played Jamaican music throughout their lives. They all played in the mento and ska scenes before Perry constructed them into his house band. The roots of dub lie in the Barrett brothers' extremely tight bass and drum lines that allowed Tubby to cut and manipulate the tracks effectively. Without the Barrett brothers, dub would have been extremely limited.

Social 3

The 1972 election in Jamaica was a pivotal point in the way that musicians and the populace viewed the government. Since independence in 1962, the conservative JLP had remained in power. The Jamaican Labour Party was in control for the first ten years of independence and was the capitalist and more conservative party. Founded in 1943 and led by Alexander Bustamante, it was the party in power during the gaining of independence. This was, and still is, the party of control over the individual, and the growth of the party is fixated on the ways that the government will sustain safety and control of the population. This government dictated a philosophy of life that matched with the corporate control of society. This was distinctly different from the working-class ideals in Jamaica, but the party won on the premise of separation. After Bustamante's stroke in 1964, he left politics but kept his title as party head. Donald Sangster took over as acting prime minister but died of a brain haemorrhage shortly after winning the election.

The other side of Jamaican politics is the People's National Party, the oldest political party in Jamaica, founded in 1938 by the Honorable Osmond Theodore Fairclough. He recruited Norman Manley to run the party and held a majority of the seats in parliament from 1955 to 1962. The party is based in democratic socialism and is currently led by Peter Phillips. They lost to the JLP in the election after independence and this shifted the political climate in the nation. It was not until Michael Manley arrived that the party gained influence.

Michael Manley took control of the PNP in 1969 and began reaching out to the people with a more populist message. Katz

(2000) discussed this in his work as well: 'He toured the country with a musical bandwagon, supported by Clancy Eccles, Bob Marley, and others, sporting a "Rod of Correction" said to have been given to him by Haile Selassie' (150). This allowed him to gain many followers. Hugh Shearer took over the JLP and lost the election, for the first time, to the PNP in 1972. Shearer's followers went into hiding and, as Roy Black (2011) discusses the musical reaction in the *Gleaner*, Jamaica's main newspaper, 'Junior Byles joined the fray in the 70s as well with "Pharaoh Hiding" – a direct reference to former Prime Minister Hugh Shearer, whose supporters went into hiding following his "dethronement"' (n.pag.).

For Perry, this also created an opportunity to produce music that supported the running of Manley. 'King of Babylon' and 'Pharaoh Hiding' were voiced by Junior Byles and became minor hits surrounding the election. 'King of Babylon' and its instrumental version 'Nebuchadnezzar' were recorded prior to the Black Ark opening at Randy's by the Impact All Stars and featured Lloyd Parks on bass. Perry was influential on Parks' bass playing and utilised his phrasings in a much different way from before. The blending of music and politics increased in this phase and continued with many other producers and musicians writing for Manley.

This was not the first time that Perry had influenced politics with his music. Leading up to Jamaican independence in the early 1960s, Perry worked with Coxsone Dodd to produce ska songs demanding and celebrating independence. 'By the dawning of Jamaican independence, Lee Perry had already brought Coxsone considerable success by insisting that he record the Maytals, a vocal trio consisting of Frederick "Toots" Hibbert, Nathaniel "Jerry" Matthias and Ralhus "Raleigh" Gordon' (Katz 2000: 177). The first song 'Hallelujah' went to number one in Jamaica and many more hits followed.

Out of these hits, Perry developed his studio and expanded his relationships with musicians in Jamaica.

> With the creation of what would eventually be known as the Black Ark, reggae music would be ushered into a new era, and the freedom brought by his studio premises would see Perry continuing to progress in his individual and unpredictable manner'.
>
> (Katz 2000: 179)

His Black Ark studio was built in 1973 behind his family home in the Washington Gardens neighbourhood of Kingston. This was a low-end studio with only a four-track recorder and a used mixing board. With this lower-level technology, Perry made it work and created some of the biggest and most interesting sounds to have ever come out of Jamaica. In Roy Ascott's (2000) work, *Art, technology, Consciousness: Mind @ Large*, Perry states:

> I see the studio must be like a living thing, a life itself. The machine must be live and intelligent. Then I put my mind into the machine and the machine perform reality. Invisible thought waves – you put them into the machine by sending them through the controls and the knobs or you jack it into the jack panel. The jack panel is the brain itself, so you got to patch up the brain and make the brain a living man, that the brain can take what you sending into it and live.
>
> (cited in Ascott 2000: 120)

The concept of technology as a 'living thing' frames the viewpoint of Perry and is what makes his compositions and soundscapes come to life themselves in the recording. This is also what many people first think of when discussing dub, the movement and 'strangeness' of the track of music that was done by the engineer and producer. In viewing the technology as living entities, Perry creates a new living thing with each song that he touches. Even in today's contemporary world of computer-based recording, this can be heard in songs produced with Perry.

Many recording engineers and producers added effects to tracks to enhance the singer's voice or the way the instruments blended before the creation of the dub. The importance here is that these previous engineers were doing so to enhance the quality of the original track. For dub, this is not the case. The engineer and producer become the main element in the track. They assert themselves fully into the mix. Before dub, the goal of the engineer was to remain anonymous and to let the track stand alone, away from their work. Erik Davis (2008) also suggests that: 'At a time when roots reggae was proclaiming a literally religious mythos of folk-cultural authenticity, dub subtly called it into question by dematerializing and eroding the integrity of singers and song' (63). Dub brought the engineer and producer to the front and demanded, through music, that the audience pay attention to them.

The shift of the engineer from quiet scientist behind the mixing board to the focal point of the music begins here with Tubby and Perry. This record, and the work by Tubby, reconstructed what people thought of studio engineers. In previous re-productions, it did not matter to the public who the engineer was. Now, the engineer became the focal point, and the musicians were relegated to the background. The tracklist for the original release has shifted with the rerelease but was A1 'Black Panta', A2 'V/S Panta Rock', A3 'Kasha Skank', A4 'Elephant Rock', A5 'African Skank', A6, 'Dreamland Skank', A7 'Jungle Jim', B1 'Drum Rock', B2 'Dub Organiser', B3 'Lovers Skank', B4 'Mooving Skank', B5 'Apeman Skank', B6 'Jungle Fever' and B7 'Kaya Skank'.

Timbre 3

The first track, originally titled 'Black Panta', A1, and re-released as 'Blackboard Jungle Dub-ver 1', opens with a callout to the listeners to 'just be humble' and then goes into an ethereal mix on the 'Bucky Skank' riddim. 'Bucky Skank' was originally released in 1973 on the Down Town label as a single with 'Yucky Skank' on the B-side. The original riddim has Perry voicing and DJing over the riddim and is an excellent version. The original does not have a flute line and does not have as many effects added to it compared to the dub track. The timbre of this song here is centred on the drums with insertions of a horn line on the flute. This track differs in timbre as the high-pitched flute is centred here running the melody across the bass and drums. Perry uses delay throughout the track, even on the opening 'whoosh' vocal line. There is also a large amount of echo on the drums that add to the spacey feel.

In the middle of the track, Perry drops the horn line out and adds in more vocal stylings filtered with delay and echo to make it sound as if a siren is going off. The bass and drums propel the track and allow the horn line to be manipulated with this delay. While the horn line is manipulated, the snare drum is mixed to sound like gunshots and the entire track floats on the bass and drums.

The original guitar line is also manipulated in this version to become something that is barely recognisable as a guitar. In the 'Bucky Skank' track, the guitar line slides cleanly up the neck and sounds like a guitar. It is an amazing move recording wise as it is not note based but sonic, even in the original version. In this track, it is manipulated to sound like a siren.

The second track on the original release was a dub of the first titled 'Version Panta Rock', A2. The timbre here is lower due to the use of a trombone instead of flute and a faster tempo to the overall track. This version has the trombone player soloing over the main track but still fixates on the bass and drums as they propel the song. The mix goes between channels in both tracks as the drums and bass feature in the left channel where the additions play out in the right. By doing so, a DJ could remove one or the other while the record was playing and create their own version in the dance hall.

Rhythmic interplay 3
The third track 'Khasha Macka', A3, begins with a call out to the DJs who chat too much over the track. The vocal states to put the bass on top and let me do my thing. Then the song features the drum and bass, but the rhythmic interplay of the track is important here and comes through with the guitar and piano chucka. The melody is carried with a melodica line, and there is an extremely slight piano line in the background of the mix. The track also has a vocal line that was mixed very low here. The bass is on top of the mix, creating a heavy but syncopated sound.

This rhythmic interplay is used around the three-minute mark when Perry stops and restarts the track on the beat. This created a push-pull feel in the track and focuses the sound onto the way the guitar and piano stress the beat. While the first two tracks contain more melody, 'Khasha Macka' delivers a bass-heavy tone while syncopating the beat.

The fourth track 'Elephant Rock', A4, takes the original song 'You Can Run' by the Hurricanes and mixes the guitars and additional drums highest in the track. The original horn line is left on the track and heard in places throughout the song, but the emphasis here is on the drums and the rhythmic interplay of the guitars. The bass is also featured after the horn intro along with the auxiliary percussion of the congas. The stick lead of the guitar becomes prominent as well and continues to push the track with its rhythmic interplay.

Re-production 3
On 'African Skank', A5, the original song 'Place Called Africa' by Junior Byles is reconstructed completely to form this dub version. The guitar and piano are removed and come into the song

sporadically to emphasise the bass line. The bass and drums are the feature here and the way that Perry inserted the guitar and piano add to the re-production of the song. It begins with the original melody line to establish what the song is and then removes everything except the drums and bass. This creates a timbre that fixates on the lower end of the spectrum and allows the song to move without anything but the bass.

The original vocal track is very faint in the background and the piano and melody line come in on the right channel only. The listener can hear the moments where Perry pushed the fader up on the guitar and piano to demonstrate the re-production of the sound.

This focus on constructing the track also happens on the next song, 'Dreamland Skank', A6. Originally by the Wailers, the song has been completely constructed around the bass line and where the piano is inserted. The piano and guitar are only briefly at the beginning of the song to set it up and then quickly removed to feature the bass and drums. The snare drum has an echo placed on it as well to give the song a different feel. By doing so, the drums become a part of the bass line and are blended into the lower frequencies of the track. In the original song, the snare pops to propel the vocal line. Here it blends with the bass line and swirls throughout the track.

The last song on side one is 'Jungle Jim', A7, which reconstructs 'Pop Goes the Weasel' into a spaced-out dub. The track keeps the original melody in the sax and then continues with drum and bass leading the way. A small skank in the guitar is mixed up to accent the rhythm, but the bass carries the song. The bass line even plays a counter melody and creates a song in the main section of the track. The re-production behind the mixing board comes through in the ways that the guitar and sax are added throughout the track. The bass line guides the track, but the guitar and sax punch through the song to set the framework and give the dub life.

Timbre 4

The B-side opens with a growl from Perry and one of the creepiest toned versions of the 'Fever' riddim called 'Drum Rock', B1. This song demonstrates the definition of the timbre of dub. The drum and bass are extremely high in the mix and everything else is secondary. As the bass line continues, there are keyboard swells and sirens that have been added to give the track a spaced-out feel. In the left channel, vocal breaths are added and in the right bubbles and other sound effects are created through modified vocal tracks. Reverb and delay are consistent elements in the track, but the bass line stays high in the mix and the drums drive it. The entire track has a dark tone that creates an ominous feel and even cuts out to give space to the effects towards the end of the song before ending with the bass line and a rush of delayed sound.

'Dub Organiser', B2, opens with Dillinger's original vocal chat and continues to use it as the intro of the track but then drops it out completely to focus on the bass line. The re-production of this track is extremely interesting as the vocal line is used as a head in a jazz tune. It surrounds the main bass line in the middle of the song. The timbre completely shifts because of this to the bass. This focus keeps the respect to the original but gives Perry room to add sounds and other effects to the mix. The way that the bass is set in the mix gives the track its timbre and is almost overbearing in parts. In the middle of the track, the bass and drums are all alone in the mix with a very faint sound of the melody line in the extreme background of the track. Then the vocal chat comes back in with the horn line to end the song.

The next track, 'Lover's Skank', B3, takes 'To Be A Lover' by Chenley Duffus and strips everything out of it except the drum and bass. The bass is mixed so high on this track that it distorts, taking a sweet love song and completely changing the tone. You can hear the piano line in the background of the mix, and it comes in and out through the track, but the focus on the bass defines the song. Here is one of the most accurate depictions of the timbre of dub on any record. It is simplistic and basic but resonates the tone throughout the body and gives the listener a descent into the darker sound of the bass. By mixing the bass so high that it distorts in the speakers, the sound is completely washed in dark tones. The drums have reverb on them to add to this wash of sound and the keyboard line that comes in is also affected to create a spacey tone.

Rhythmic interplay 4

On 'Mooving Skank', B4, Perry recreates the Wailers' 'Keep on Moving' as a dub classic as well. This track could also fit into the timbre section, but this song keeps the rhythmic interplay of the guitar and more of the original parts. The re-production of the track is also extremely interesting as the main song was well known. The track opens with the same guitar opening and then immediately drops out to drum and bass. This gives the original song a darker tone, but the bass is not mixed to distort it but to propel the track. The rhythmic interplay here is mainly in the drumline and the way that the original drum part is used. Around 1:34 in the track, the guitar and piano line come in to syncopate the song again. The original song is restated through this rhythmic interplay, but the track fixates on the bass and drums.

'Apeman Skank', B5, also shares this rhythmic interplay in the drums. The original melody is stretched here and placed in the back of the mix to fixate the track on the drums. The bass is also high in the mix, but Perry plays with the percussive elements here and syncopates the drumline with other percussions to give the track a drive that others do not have on the record. There are also stops and starts of the drumline overall. This track is a version of 'Caveman Skank' and uses percussion as the focus as the bass line is very simplistic here. This allows the high hat to cut through the mix much more and to push the track with the rhythmic interplay instead of the melody. There is a melody in the bass that is used to create the start and stop in the middle of the track, but the drums are the focus here.

Re-production 4

The record closes with 'Jungle Fever', B6 and 'Kaya Skank', B7. Both tracks are versions of songs that had become popular in the dance halls. 'Jungle Fever' is a version of 'Water Pump' that removed the vocals that Perry had originally added and 'Kaya Skank' is a version of the Wailers' song 'Kaya'. In 'Jungle Fever', the bass line again drives the song by setting up the rhythm in the beginning and then Perry constructs the tracks following the bass. The drums cut in and out while the bass is mixed loudly enough to distort. The main organ line in the chorus is used, along with the guitar, to signify the original song, but the bass and drums drive this track and the additional percussion adds to the feel of the modifications. This riddim would go on to be used many times in popular music, but this is the definitive dub version as the re-production of the track forms the song.

On 'Kaya Skank', the Wailers' vocal line is removed, and the original track is reused. Both were Perry productions and contain signature elements of the work that the Wailers did with him. The dub is an example of the constructive elements of dub. It begins with the guitar and piano in the mix setting up the melody and then continues with the bass at the top of the mix. The drums are extremely high in the mix as well, with the high-hat swirling around the beat to syncopate the song. The piano and guitar come in during the transition to solidify the song and then are removed quickly to keep the timbre. The record closes with one of the most successful songs going through the elements of dub. The way that the melody is inserted throughout the track is interesting as it is not always in expected places but comes in at odd intervals.

Completion 3

Blackboard Jungle Dub is a key element in the culture of dub. The development of the dub genre in reggae begins here. Each track resonates with the qualities of the style and the way that Perry put the entire record together would go on to influence reggae and Jamaican music to this day. The argument of which record was first is not as relevant here as is the effect that this record would have on the culture and society in Jamaica.

> Dub albums would gradually become more common in Jamaica, and would eventually be made off the island, its practices slowly filtering into other forms of popular music, but *Blackboard Jungle Dub* shows Perry again as a true innovator in his field.
> (Katz 2000: 178)

This innovation began the focus on the engineer and producer in dub. Before Perry's album, the producer may have been famous, but the engineer was not. Perry and Tubby changed this with *Blackboard Jungle Dub* and began a new genre of sonic manipulation that resisted pure commodity. The tracks on this album are not just meant to be sold but are artistic statements that resonate throughout the culture. 'It also emphasizes the highly skilled musicianship of the Upsetters, and shows just how creative Perry's approach to rhythm could be' (Katz 2000: 179). Perry took the beginnings of dub and the changes that can be heard on *Java, Java, Java, Java* and *Aquarius Dub* and inserted his sound into the track. Instead of just hearing what was done to the original song, now you could listen for what the engineer had added.

This was a drastic shift in dub culture and one that represents the distinction between version and dub.

The importance of the engineer becoming relevant in the discussion of music to popular fans occurs here as well. In previous recordings, the singer and musicians were the focus and what the engineer did to the track was only discussed by theorists and hardcore fans of the groups. It could be argued that the discussion and focus on producers and engineers begin with dub and the music that was created here. There were many famous producers beforehand, but the focus on them was not as prevalent as it was after the music of dub.

Michael Manley winning the election and taking over the government changed the way people saw the link between music and politics in Jamaica. Lee 'Scratch' Perry was a key player in this shift and gained an immense amount of popularity and support through doing so. With Manley's 'rod of correction' and Perry's 'Pharaoh in Hiding', the dance hall and sound systems became even more rooted in political struggle. The music of the streets, with dub as a part of that, became political. Social class politics framed the sound and the darker timbre of the bass lines in dub found a place with the people. The shift from the brighter sounds of ska and rocksteady came in through version and dub. This began with Thompson and Morris and was furthered by Tubby and Perry to bring these darker tones to the people.

Perry was consistently involved with political music and the creation of sounds based on the people. Dub became linked to working-class socialist ideals through Perry's influence. These sounds can be heard on this record and begin the rise of the engineer and producer as focal points in Jamaican music. *Blackboard Jungle Dub* is a complete album that sonically linked tracks to create an entire dub album that represented the politics of the lower classes in Jamaica at the time.

Chapter 4
The Message Spreads: Prince Buster and the Sound of Jamaica

My father, Prince Buster, is Jamaica's first superstar. Because of him Jamaica has a sound.
                              Sultan Ali (aka Danny Buster) (2018)

Another one of the often-mentioned records to hold the claim of the first dub album is *The Message Dubwise* by Prince Buster, in 1972. Prince Buster's position in the music industry allowed this record to be viewed as the first dub release. Having been very successful in the previous ska scene and having charted the first Jamaican song in the British charts with 'Al Capone' in 1965, Buster shifted through the early reggae scene by recording slack[4] songs and then produced his dub sound. Prince Buster, Cecil Bustamante Campbell OD, was one of the first to champion a sound system in the 1960s as well with his Voice of the People sound system. All of these elements came together in the release of *The Message Dubwise* and situate this album as one of the key records in dub and Jamaican popular music. His songs and style were always at the front of the Jamaican sound. From the ska era hits 'Madness', 'Wash Wash', 'One Step Beyond' and 'Al Capone', through the rocksteady era with hits like 'Shaking up Orange Street', and 'Judge Dread', to *The Message Dubwise*, Buster's recordings were influential in defining sound not only in Jamaica but also throughout the world. The way that Campbell captured the trends of music on the island from the beginning of his time as a producer allowed him to take the lead. His sound system was extremely influential in the shift from boogie-woogie and swing music to ska, and his record label, Blue Beat, helped to establish the Jamaican sound in England and other parts of the world. His later releases on Melodisc, who released *The Message Dubwise*, continued to spread the word.

The Prince Buster All Stars, who included many of the most famous musicians in Jamaica at the time, performed all the tracks on this record. Cecil Bustamente Campbell (Vocals, Direction), Val Bennet, Tommy McCook, Roland Alphonso (saxophones), Raymond Harper and Baba Brooks (trumpets), Junior Nelson and Rico Rodriguez (trombones), Ernest Ranglin and Jerry Haines (guitar), Gladstone Anderson (piano) and Arkland 'Drumbago' Parks (drums) formed the group. These names are mentioned in previous chapters and include musicians that continue to play Jamaican music today. The group laid and continued the foundation for the sound of dub, and this recording would spread the culture of dub to other countries and locales in the world.

Figure 4.1: Amplifier in Tony Meyer's yard. Photo: Courtesy of Cassandra Abbey (2019).

Many of the musicians were in the band the Skatalites previously and were farmed by Prince Buster for this record. The Skatalites legacy in Jamaican music cannot be overstated as they were the first band to play ska. Mostly coming out of the Alpha Boys School, Tommy McCook, Rico Rodriguez and others formed the group and went through the program at Alpha. From the Skatalites website (2018), 'the band became legendary, backing all the developing artists of the day, such as Toots and The Maytals, Prince Buster and "The Wailing Wailers" featuring Bob Marley, Peter Tosh and Bunny Wailer' (n.pag.). Although the entire group is not present on *The Message Dubwise*, they were well known by Prince Buster and he used musicians from the Skatalites often in his sessions.

There is a discernible difference between this album and the others mentioned in this book. This difference comes about in the way that Prince Buster produced and chose the mixing style. Carlton Lee was the engineer on the record, and it was recorded at Dynamics studio. The addition of Big Youth's voice on the last track would go on to influence the DJ culture that the sound systems had been displaying for years previously. This was, as stated on the back of the record: 'Raw-Pure-Not Diluted – the Jamaican Rhythm Expresses the Feeling of the Jamaican People'. David Katz (2012) quotes Prince Buster stating:

> When I say *The Message*, a lot of people don't understand what I ah talk 'bout. At that time in my life, a lot of things happen to me, and I send a message to some serious people. The music was one thing, but there was sublime messages them must understand. You say them [rival producers] make dub; it's hard for me to tell you what day them make their dub, and I don't have the dates to tell you exactly whether it was them first, but I know a lot of people tell me that *The Message* was the first good dub that them hear.
>
> (n.pag.)

The tracklisting for the album is A1 'Swing Low', A2 'Sata A Masa Gana', A3 'Java Plus', A4 'The Message', A5 'Mississippi', B1 'Saladin', B2 'Why Am I Treated So Bad', B3 'Jet Black', B4 'Black Harem' and B5 'Big Youth'.

One of the most profound differences in this album is the way that the flute and melodica are used throughout most of the tracks.

This creates a feeling of the higher resonance floating on top of the bass and drums and allows for the melody to be repeated. The addition of the flute evokes a more Eastern sound than previous dub records. This would become Prince Buster's style of dub along with the minimal use of effects. This differentiates from the style of Lee 'Scratch' Perry and the other forerunners of the culture and led to Prince Buster gaining immense popularity because of it.

The Message Dubwise shares elements of both the version and dub genres of reggae and is a culmination of the original sound of dub. By using the original song as a referent on every track, the listener is given a starting point to latch onto. This reflects back to the sound of *Java, Java, Java, Java* and *Aquarius Dub* and situates the album in the version genre as it was more of a reflection on the producer and his reuse of the tracks for monetary and artistic gain. The way that Lee mixed the record is also interesting and artistic as the use of the flute and the fader moves create space to add a different feeling from other dub albums. These moves, particularly the insertion of the flute, place the record into the dub genre as well. The main distinction here is that the producer, Prince Buster, is the main selling point of the record. Lee is barely known or mentioned in connection with the album. As the engineer on the record, his mixing and insertions can be heard, but the reason that this record was successful was because of Prince Buster producing it.

The difference between this record and Perry's *Blackboard Jungle Dub* is much more than just what is inserted or not into the sound. This record upholds the previous notions of who is at the forefront of the record. The producer is the key here as it was Buster's name who sold this record. The engineer is relegated to the background as in previous studio recordings. This was also an attempt to ride off of the popularity of dub in Jamaica at the time. Buster was extremely good at knowing what trends and sounds were being followed by the people and was extremely successful because of it.

The record was mixed at Dynamic Sounds studio by Carlton Lee. Dynamic Sounds, previously West Indies Recording Limited (WIRL), was bought by Byron Lee from Edward Seaga after a fire had decimated the studio. Lee brought it back to life and the studio became the place to record for hits. Carlton Lee was the engineer and worked on many of the most famous records by Derrick

Morgan and Byron Lee and the Dragonaires. The studio became so well known that the Rolling Stones recorded their *Goats Head Soup* album there in 1973.

Due to sharing the principles of both genres of dub, this album holds an interesting space in the discussion of commodity culture. Prince Buster began his career working for Coxsone Dodd and listening to other sound systems to steal their songs and specials. He then broke away and began his own system, Voice of the People, and gained success through cutthroat means. Prince Buster knew what it took to be successful in Jamaica and did it. He was influential in creating the sound of Jamaica and created the culture that is still present today. *The Message Dubwise* was produced after he became famous and, in some ways, to catch onto a developing trend in the culture. His 'reputation as a specialist' went before him as he produced the record and Carlton Lee fell to the background. This is a producer record but with the sound of dub that resonated with the people.

This album does fall into the 'culture commodity' area that Horkheimer and Adorno discuss. The commodity was created within the culture, and the autonomy of the specialist was used to sell the product. Some of the songs, especially 'Sata A Masa Gana', became hit songs and riddims that influenced many artists around the world. Without Prince Buster's name on the record, the album would not have gained as many listeners. Although this is a commodity of culture, Prince Buster was a part of creating the culture and sound of Jamaica. The version and dub genres of reggae blend here to create an album that was shared across the world and one that inspired many, including the 2-Tone label in England.

In our contemporary world, there is a need to define culture and self. This need leads many people to discover different types and styles of music. For Prince Buster, this need framed the basis of his productions, to give Jamaica its music and to share it with the world. In many cases, music is used to define self or to create and represent a culture. This is due to the duration of time and the ways in which the world is situated in such duration. There are many people who discuss how the world is constructed and/or viewed. The suggestion here is based on Gaston Bachelard's work on duration and time.

The duration of the songs on this album, and the connections that were developed because of it, created a resonance of Jamaican music and dub. The culture shifted because of this record. This led to a continuing focus on dub and the music of Jamaica by the rest of the world. In *The Dialectic of Duration*, Bachelard (2000) states: 'the phenomena of duration are constructed by rhythms, rhythms that are by no means necessarily grounded on an entirely uniform and regular time' (xiv). This phenomena are referencing how we live in the world and how we construct self. It is discussing how the duration of a sound, or something that is constructed, is based on the rhythm and rhythms involved. Bachelard is determined to assert that because everything creates a vibration, that vibration must contain a rhythm and structure. 'Events do not therefore settle along the length of duration like direct and natural gains. They need to be ordered in an artificial system –a rational or social system – that gives them meaning and a date' (Bachelard 2000: 53). For Jamaican music, *The Message Dubwise* reflects this re-production and the rhythms fixate on the sound of the people.

The distinction here relies on the way that this album has affected multiple genres of music and sounds. The duration does not just lie in the music itself, but in the entire album. Bachelard again states:

> If we go on to add that in the same way melody 'can be compared to a living being', we have created a whole family, an entire closed cycle of metaphors that will constitute the language of continuity, the song and indeed the lullaby of continuity. Tranquil duration, life that is well balanced, music that sweeps us along, sweet reverie, clear and fruitful thought, all of these offer us experiences 'proving' time to be continuous.
>
> (2000: 53)

Although Bachelard is speaking of existence itself and how to construct it, the argument here is that *The Message Dubwise* offers a 'music that sweeps us along' and one that 'proves' this continuity of time.

Bachelard states that all music does this, that music is a metaphor for existence, and discusses the ways in which duration can be comingled with melody and time. Dub, the entire genre, reflects this and becomes almost a direct representation of this with its manipulations of sound. Buster used these connections to influence the people of Jamaica and to expand that sound to the world.

'It is not *heard* straightaway, and it is often the recognition of a theme that makes us aware of melodic continuity' (Bachelard 2000: 109–10, emphasis added). This 'recognition of a theme' creates the basis for many of Prince Buster's dub tracks on this album. There is a significant use of the methods represented in the rhythm genre throughout the album that connects the listener to the original song.

This connection also plays out when looking at dub as a type of 'groove music' as discussed by Mark Abel (2016).

> It is feasible to argue that temporal regularity found in the best instances of groove music qualifies as genuine mimesis because it displays both of the necessary criteria. First, it takes as its starting point the temporal reality of the world as it is [...]. Second, however, the best popular music does not simply incorporate clock time into its forms, but through a process of mimesis seeks to humanize a temporality which has become rigid and reified'
> (Abel 2016: 175)

His discussion is framed around a critique of Adorno's conception of rigid rhythmic interplay relating to capitalist ideals. In Abel's view, the groove allows for a reflection of the world and an ability to change and shift the contemporary capitalist society. 'On this basis, the groove-based temporality of the best Western popular music can be recognized as a mimetic response to the highly measured temporality of the contemporary world, capable of effecting a critique of it' (Abel 2016: 175).

Both Bachelard and Abel discuss how rhythm and groove have become synonymous with existence. Helping to define and place our reality into a structure allows us to deconstruct and form opinions based on these structures of sound and vibration. Through these theorists, dub music becomes a way to create social structure, culture and self in many different versions and styles dependent on the listener.

Prince Buster's entire catalog can be viewed as a critique of the society that he was involved with. His songs and productions were rooted in the people of Jamaica, and his focus was on developing purely Jamaican music. Edward Seaga, before becoming Prime Minister, supported Buster's efforts to stake a claim on the music of Jamaica. The groove led to a distinct and lasting change to the music and one that influenced the world. *The Message Dubwise* is a demonstration of this groove and is a mimesis of the Jamaican people.

Social 4

Prince Buster was a leader in what would become the sound of Jamaica. His sound system, Voice of the People, was the first to play ska and specifically Jamaican styles of music. The sound systems that were around at the time were playing r&b and other forms of American music like big band swing for their listeners. Buster made his sound about Jamaica. Donna Hope (2018) discussed the influence of music in Jamaica on her growing up: 'It sounded far more to me than just noise, it sounded to me, back then as a teenager, as a young adult, as an aspect of our lives. Music was always so integrated into our daily lives'. This is not an uncommon statement from others in Jamaica as well. The use of music in daily life is something that informs many Jamaicans.

This integration forms the connection between Jamaican people and the culture at the time. Being surrounded by music allowed the duration of the sounds to become part of the populace. When the music reflects that populace and embraces the working-class ideals that many were living with, it changes the culture. Dr. Hope's discussion of 'more than just noise' relates to many who have grown up surrounded by music. The music becomes a mimesis of the society at the time. The ways that this occurs lie in the developments of Prince Buster.

His boxing career in his early life left his hands too damaged to get a visa for work in the United States. In *Ska: An Oral History*, Heather Augustyn (2010) states: 'So, Prince Buster turned to the wealth of local artists and claims it was during this time that he created the distinctive ska sound, a claim that many artists make' (25). The importance of this cannot be understated as the shift was the first in many for Prince Buster. His entire career was focused on hearing new sounds and framing them through Jamaica. According to Sultan Ali (2018), aka Danny Buster, 'he always said, "I like to be different"'. In *Bass Culture: When Reggae was King*, Prince Buster tells Lloyd Bradley (2000):

> When I couldn't get the visa to run up and down to America like Duke Reid and Coxsone, it knock me back. I had already

demolished the other two in a street clash, I have the number
one set, the number one disc jockey in Count Machuki, but
I know I couldn't keep up any challenge if I had to rely on rhythm
and blues. I have to have my own music. [...] Radio stations in
Jamaica – our stations – that were supposed to represent us the
Jamaican people – were dominated by American rhythm and
blues, and even though I loved it so much I knew it had to go.

(57)

It was this drive to be innovative that led to the creation of a
Jamaican sound and is what would lead Prince Buster to change
the way people outside of Jamaica heard the country's music.

A significant example of this, and one that is often discussed, is the
song 'Oh, Carolina'. This song was released on Buster's record label
Buster Wild Bells and recorded at RJR Studios in 1960. It was written
by the Folkes Brothers and is important as it is the first time in history
that Nyabinghi drumming was recorded on a record by members of
the Count Ossie group. Prince Buster brought Rastafarians into the
studio, as he was becoming more spiritual, against many people's
advice, and the sound of the chanting and drumming on the track
changed the way people viewed Jamaican music.

The song became a hit in Jamaica and then was released in
the United Kingdom on Melodisc, who released it on Blue Beat
records. 'Oh, Carolina' would go on to become a hit in the United
Kingdom in 1961 as well and helped to establish the 'sound of
Jamaica'. 'It is difficult to gauge the importance of Prince Buster's
"Oh Carolina." While in terms of actual musical re-production it
probably wasn't that influential, as a piece of cultural legislation
it was enormous' (Bradley 2000: 61). This drew many musicians
and producers to Buster's studio who wanted the 'sound' that he
was getting. 'Buster's Boop Boop Beat' would become legendary
in Jamaica. It also led to a change in the social nature of Jamaican
music as the sound of ska began. Buster would then become a part
of the shift to rocksteady, reggae and eventually dub. Utilising
studios around Kingston but primarily Dynamics, Federal and
RJR, he changed the way that people thought of Jamaican music.

Sultan Ali also discussed some of the first things that inspired
him from the music. As a youth, Ali would collect soda and beer
bottles from the dance-hall party that Voice of the People was
holding for return and reuse. Prince Buster wrote and recorded

the song 'Danny, Dane, and Lorraine' about his children, the first 'Royal Family' in Jamaica. Ali recounted the first sound that he remembers being inspired by as being the sound of the two-track reel-to-reel recorder in the studio with Carlton Lee as the engineer and his father producing (Ali 2018). This sound would also go on to influence the entire spectrum of Jamaican music.

An important difference, during this early time in Jamaican music, is that each producer had their own distinct sound. Prince Buster's sound was his own, and he utilised musicians in a different way from other producers of the time. The bass tone was often met with horns and higher-pitched instruments in a way that allowed both to become focal points. This blending of tones can be heard on his dub album but also throughout his recordings. The difference also lies in how technology was used to create these sounds.

In contemporary music, technology creates a lack of difference and creativity in some places, particularly the popular market. In contrast, the forms of technology that were being introduced in Jamaica were used as part of the creative process and helped to innovate and create new sounds. This innovation is still happening today, but the ease of recording and producing has taken away some of the creative elements. According to Ali, 'technology has made things lack feeling' (2018). It is this feeling that comes across in *The Message Dubwise*.

The technology that was available to Buster was very different from the technology used by Tubby and Lee 'Scratch' Perry. Buster had access to top of the line studio technology and made good use of it. While Tubby and Perry used what they could borrow or purchased used, Buster was at a technological advantage. Buster also was not as familiar with this technology as Morris, Thompson and Tubby. Carlton Lee was more familiar and his effort on this record is still recognised less than Buster's.

Timbre 5

The differences in this album come through in the use of timbre. This is not the heavy bass and drums of other dub albums. It does contain these elements, as the tracks discussed below display, but the concept of floating a higher-pitched melody over the bass and drums is prominent here. The title track of the album is where the standard use of bass and drums is heard first. With 'The Message', A4, Prince Buster began the track with the melody and then removes it to feature the drums and bass with only slight guitar in the mix. The stick lead of the guitar and the rhythmic interplay are mixed into the track, but the bass and drums carry the song. It is interesting that in developing his own style, Buster chose to name the record after a song that is like others in dub culture.

This timbre also appears in 'Mississippi', A5. Here the same framework operates but the track begins with a roll on a cowbell that comes in throughout the track. The bass and drums are mixed very high in the track to where the bass distorts in places. This centres the track into dub culture and stands out within it for the use of the cowbell. As the track begins, the horn line is used to let the audience become familiar with the song and then it is cut quickly to begin the focus on the bass. There is a small break in the middle of the song where the melody comes in again, but this is cut up by using the bass as the main melody line. The horn line comes through a bit in the mix during this part, but it is bleed through from the original track. There is also a small trumpet part that comes through towards the end of the track, but it is non-distinct as the bass is mixed extremely high.

Another track on the reverse side of the record displays this type of timbre and mixing style. In 'Jet Black' B3, the track begins with a small part of the original melody and then continues with the bass as the focus. The original vocal line can be heard bleeding through, but the bass is on top of the mix and, with the drums, carries the song. In this track, there are also moments when Buster removes everything but the drums to keep the timbre in the lower register. The organ bubble is used very sparingly here as well to let the listener orientate themselves back to the melody.

Rhythmic interplay 5

Much like the timbre of this album, the rhythmic interplay is also used in a slightly different manner than other albums in dub culture. The rhythmic interplay dominates the tracks 'Why Am I Treated So Bad', B2, and 'Black Harem', B4. Both tracks were hit songs prior to them being dubbed. Lyn Taitt and the Jets recorded 'Why Am I Treated So Bad' as an upbeat instrumental ska song and Prince Buster shifted the feel completely to make the song darker and fixated on the bass. The rhythmic interplay is still resonant here and is what drives the song, but the organ line over that is like the original and gives the audience the orientation needed.

The chord structure and other parts of the song are similar, but the track has been slowed down immensely and the rhythmic interplay of the guitar and organ dominate the mix. The song is slowed down so much in the second half of the track that the chords are forced into a different pattern. The horns in this part are morphed as well. The drums are also extremely loud in this mix with the addition of cowbell, wood block and bells. By fixating the track at a slower speed and making it darker by removing almost all the horns, Buster and Lee created a new song with the rhythmic interplay in the lead.

This also occurs in 'Black Harem' B4 that takes a hit song 'Stick by Me' by Delroy Wilson, John Holt and other vocalists and transforms it into a dark dub. The dub is slowed down, and the rhythmic interplay in the guitar carries this track. The addition of a guiro to the track also allows the rhythmic interplay to be the focus of the dub version. By doing so, the original love song is transformed into a darker sound, but one that is syncopated in the same manner as the original.

Re-production 5

The other three albums that are discussed previously in this writing are filled with elements of re-production, but for dub culture, *The Message Dubwise* gained the most popularity and spread the culture into other countries around the world. The suggestion here is that this album does not differentiate in drastic ways that disorient the audience and that the main re-production of the tracks is important but limited. With the addition of Big Youth on the final track of the record, Prince Buster helped to introduce the culture of the dance hall and sound system to the world. The other tracks are imperative to the constructive element as well.

The album opens with a shout-out to the audience about who is in control and then breaks into A1 'Swing Low'. The track focuses on the melody line that is created by the bass. The flute is also used here, which is different from other dub tracks as it comes in and out of the track more and gives the entire track a higher-pitched resonance. By beginning the album with this song, Prince Buster establishes this as a standout album that is different from the rest. The bass and drums still drive this song and keep the timbre in the lower register but the flute line, and how it is manipulated with a spring reverb, becomes the focus. By weaving the flute with the bass an interesting split occurs while listening to it as the flute somewhat floats above the bass line. There are also elements of tape delay and reverb that are used throughout the track to affect it and to situate Carlton Lee as the engineer and Buster as the producer.

The way that the guitar and these elements are used would go on to become signatures of Prince Buster's style of producing. They are more reserved than other engineers and allow for the deeper tone of the track to remain mixed with the effected flute. This style allowed for the culture of dub to reach many more people as the melody was more coherent and the tracks fixated more on the manipulation of the faders and less on the addition of other effects. 'Swing Low' demonstrates how effective this can be and starts the album off in a distinctive style.

'Sata a Masa Gana', A2 also carries this timbre by starting off with a flute line over hand drums with a slight whistle as well. The flute then goes into a solo fluttering over just the propulsion of the drums. There is another whistle and growl that comes in as well to separate the flute solo from the main flute line. The re-production of this track is interesting as the bass is very soft, comparatively, and the hand drums and flute distinguish the song. There are also many versions of this song, but none in which the flute is so prominent. By having the flute carry the track, the song takes on a new tone and makes the listener focus on the ways in which it is constructed.

On 'Java Plus', A3, the constructive element comes through as well. The song begins with a familiar Far East melody played on the guitar and then jumps into the main focal point of the song in the melodica. Here, the melodica and stick lead of the guitar frame the song, and the melodica is used as a solo instrument to construct a melody, at times even playing without anything else on the track. Then the stick lead and bass line become prominent and start trading with the melodica. The guitar also plays a chorded pattern to separate the song, and then the melodica continues to solo. This re-production is based on jazz patterns where the song is framed as head-solo-head and much like the opening track 'Swing Low' the soloist is a higher-pitched instrument.

On 'Saladin' B1, the opening track on the B-side, the re-production is also framed around a flute melody. Beginning with a cowbell hit, the flute takes the lead and, while being affected with reverb and delay, comes in and out of the track more than other dub versions. The re-production of the cowbell in this track is also very interesting as it is a high-pitched percussion element. The cowbell here pierces through in parts, and the organ swells and flute trills are heavily affected to give this track a high-pitched tone but one that is still dark and spacey. This forms the Prince Buster sound.

Then the final track of the record comes in. 'Big Youth', B5, is the feature of the album and has the DJ Big Youth chatting over different styles of riddims. This was one of the first recordings ever released where the riddims differ as the DJ stays on top of them. This track would go onto to influence hip hop and many other forms of music throughout the world by doing so. The songs that are played vary and show how a DJ could go in and out of the original vocal effectively. The representation of Jamaican popular sound system and dance-hall music starts here. Not only is this an introduction of Big Youth, it is also the beginning of the representation of this culture. The re-production of the different songs with his voice coming in and out of each one is the key to this recording and to the message that is spread.

Completion 4

In Bachelard's discussion of duration, the ways in which time and timbre intertwine to reflect existence play a large part in dub. This connection flows in each song and throughout the albums that have been discussed. *The Message Dubwise* is a representation of this 'comingling' and demonstrates how music can reflect the people. By using Jamaican musicians and recording studios, and changing the way people view Jamaican music, Prince Buster formed the basis of the 'Jamaican Sound'. The duration of this material and how it spread throughout the world created a structure and sound that is still heard today.

Bachelard (2000) also comments on the ways in which we 'accompany' music even in its simplest terms.

> It can be said that when we listen to a melody that is as linear as it is possible to be, we give it density, we *accompany* it [...]. We cannot hear its connectedness, its continuous duration, without this heterogeneous summation of sound and soul.
>
> (Bachelard 2000: 124)

This connectedness is what we hear in the works of Prince Buster.

Dub music begins in this linear fashion as it utilises the basic instruments of the song first. Both in version and dub, this minimising occurs first. Then the song is added to and reshaped by the engineer and/or producer of the track. In all the works in this study, we can see elements that tie the music to the people of Jamaica and the 'soul' of the culture. Although this happens in other forms of music, dub begins and is rooted in Jamaica. Prince Buster knew this when he created *The Message Dubwise* and this record culminates his catalog in this representation.

The mimesis of Jamaican culture and society also takes place within this album. By using sounds and styles of music that were already popular to construct this record, Prince Buster framed the music for the people and culture of Jamaica. The resonance of the bass and drums relates to the sound of the working class, and the reuse of the melody allows the people to recognise the song. By using styles that fall into both genres of reggae, version and dub, Carlton Lee and Prince Buster produced an album that reflects the culture of Jamaica.

The culture commodity of the record is also framed with the idea that it reflects the culture directly. Even though it is a product to be sold and consumed, the music on it was produced to reflect the culture. Abel (2016) states: 'It is certainly true that the grooves of popular music circulate fully within a system of commodity exchange, controlled by an industry moved solely by the logic of capital accumulation' (16). The importance here lies in the determination of Prince Buster to capture the culture. This was different from other attempts at dub but shared similar characteristics. To gain money was always the key, but this record and the argument can be extended to all of Prince Buster's catalog, attempted to give voice to the Jamaican sound.

The Message Dubwise stands as one of the most important records in Jamaican music as its influence is carried throughout the world. The mixture of both version and dub genres allowed listeners to experience dub without losing associations of the original track. The producer was at the forefront of this record, and, because of his fame, the record was a success. From his beginnings with Tom, 'The Great' Sebastian, working with Coxsone Dodd, to the Voice of the People and *The Message Dubwise*, the music that Prince Buster was a part of carried into the music culture of the world.

Chapter 5
How It All Began: King Tubby and the Sound of Dub

Figure 5.1: Amplifier in Tony Meyer's yard. Photo: Courtesy of Cassandra Abbey (2019).

Osbourne Ruddock, O.D., King Tubby, is the start of the concept and creation of dub in Jamaica. As a radio repairman, he worked on speakers and sound system components for seemingly everyone who played records in Jamaica. His creations with the mixing board, in a small studio, would go on to influence music around the world. He collaborated with many of the artists mentioned in this study and became known as the engineer to dub your sound. In 1976, *King Tubbys Meets Rockers Uptown* became the culmination of dub and contained every element of the culture and sound. The record sits in the dub genre of reggae and demonstrates how the elements of this culture came together with the engineer in control. The record became very successful featuring Augustus Pablo on melodica, piano, organ and clavinet on the record. Pablo also produced the record, which gave the record a strong starting point in the market. Ruddock began his performance career in 1958 at the age of seventeen years with Tubby's Hometown Hi-Fi and quickly became the sound to beat on the island.

Ruddock's nickname stems from his mother's surname of Tubman and his development in the industry began as he attended college for engineering and began repairing transformers around Jamaica for businesses and shops. In 'A beginner's guide to King Tubby', David Katz (2015) states: 'He began building radios from discarded parts salvaged from business rubbish tips, and soon opened an electrical repair shop at the rear of his mother's home' (n.pag.). He then created his own radio from spare parts and got a two-track tape machine and finally a record cutting machine. These machines allowed him to create acetate versions for the sound systems on the island. In doing so, he began to establish his name with the producers and musicians in Kingston. His small studio really began to produce tracks when he got an MCI mixing board in 1971 and Scully and Ampex 4 – track tape machines from Dynamic Sounds with the help of Bunny Lee. This board allowed him to control the mix and dub began under his control of the board. He turned the front room of his mother's house at 18 Dromilly Avenue, in the Waterhouse area of Kingston, into a studio, which could only mix, and began adding effects to the B-side version and rhythm that he had created for the sound systems. Phillip Mayseles (2002) states, in 'Dubbing the nation', 'Tubby brought to it his understanding of sound "inna a *scientific* sense," a feel for the way sound moves through the open air, an intimate understanding of what his people danced to, and a tinkerer's playfulness' (101, emphasis added). Tubby took the version concept and turned it into dub, thus expanding Jamaican music. He built a vocal booth in the bathroom of the house, and, from there on out, his studio became the place to voice versions and riddims.

The other extremely important piece of equipment in his studio was what was called the Dub machine. This was the dub plate cutter that was used to cut the song to the lacquer for playing in the sound system. There are claims from Tubby's brother Leslie 'Stagga' Ruddock that he sent the machine to him from America, but these are questioned. It does not matter how he got the machine, he got it and used it more successfully than others had before. In *King Tubbys: The Dub Master*, Thibault Ehrengardt (2020) suggests: 'Anyway, the *Dub machine* became a crucial part of the studio. Tubby had a Presto 6N, a portable model from 1941' (44, emphasis added). This machine became so important to the studio that engineers who messed the machine up by breaking the needle or effecting the parts were often removed from the studio immediately.

For *King Tubbys Meets the Rockers Uptown*, the tracks were recorded at Randy's studio in Kingston and were then voiced over by Pablo. The band for this album included Augustus Pablo, melodica, piano, organ and clavinet, Robbie Shakespeare and Aston Barrett bass, Carlton Barrett drums, Earl 'Chinna' Smith on guitar, Richard 'Dirty Harry' Hall saxophone, Bobby Ellis trumpet and Vincent 'Don D Junior' Gordon trombone. King Tubby and Errol Thompson mixed the album. When recording for Tubby, this group was known as the Aggrovators. The Mango label released the first single from the record in 1974 (MS-2001), and the record had the title track on the A-side and 'Baby I Love You So' as the B-side. Clocktower Records (CT-0085) and Yard Music released the full-length album and the track list for the album is A1 Keep on Dubbing, A2 Stop Them Jah, A3 Young Generation Dub, A4 Each One Dub, A5 555 Dub Street, B1 Braces Tower Dub, B2 King Tubby Meets Rockers Uptown, B3 Corner Crew Dub, B4 Say So, B5 Skanking Dub, B6 Frozen Dub and B7 (unlisted) Satta Dub.

The way that King Tubby created and manipulated his equipment formed the basis of the dub genre and of reggae. In Michael Veal's (2007) book, *Dub: Soundscapes and Shattered Rhythms* he quotes 'Computer' Paul Henton: '"There's no way you can think of dub music without thinking of King Tubbys. Because when everyone else was producing a lot of other artists and doing other things, his focus was just on pioneering that dub sound'" (116). His use of the high-pass filter and self-created spring reverb and delay influenced a countless number of musicians and fans. He created his own echo delay by passing a loop of tape over his two-track tape machine. The tape delay could be used at any time setting, and this allowed Tubby and others to stretch the feel of any sound on the track. Drums were the main instrument stretched with a tape delay and this stretching reconstructed the drums in a different way to get the listener into the rhythmic tone of the song. Spring reverb was also used to create this bouncing of the track.

Spring reverb was created, originally, through kicking or hitting a guitar amp and hearing the 'boing' of the spring within the tube of the amp. Listen to King Tubby's 'Dub You Can Feel' to experience this sound. This effect became a focal point on guitars in dub and again expanded the sound of a chord. This expansion on the minimal guitar and piano parts used in the dub created a feeling of space that enveloped the listener. The major characteristic here is in the lengthening of the sound to create a form of space and an effect of washing away the original track.

Tubby was the engineer on Lee 'Scratch' Perry's *Blackboard Jungle Dub* as well, and it is his work on this album that started the dub genre of reggae. According to Sean Williams (2012), in 'Tubby's dub style: The live art of record production':

> The two remaining constant elements therefore, that contribute to the distinctive sonic characteristics – the soundprint – of mixes made at Tubby's studio are the equipment used and the performance practice associated with the act of mixing as opposed to the original act of recording. It is worth noting that these elements are electrical and physical as opposed to being acoustic and physical, and therefore it is useful to think of King Tubby as an electronic music maker.
> (239)

Williams here suggests that Tubby was an electronic musician that links him to the contemporary producers making music with computer technology. By doing so, this suggests that King Tubby is similar to today's bedroom producer. Tubby's use of the mixing board and tape machines was much more informed than today's producers as these items required much more knowledge.

These original sound engineers were electrical engineers first and their knowledge of the workings of sound waves and machinery led to their prowess in the studio.

This concept of physical manipulation of the music through electronics is imperative to dub culture. With King Tubby, the mixing board became an instrument to use and to create with. This differed from previous albums that reused the same track to gain more exposure. This was reuse that created a new sound. The difference between playing an acoustic instrument and playing a mixing board began with Thompson, Morris and Tubby. After this occurred, the ways that engineers mixed a sound changed around the world. The 'soundprint' of the studio is also an interesting way to conceptualise the dub genre of reggae. By analysing the soundprint of the song, the engineer comes to the front of the discussion, as does the producer, and the musicians and song itself become secondary. This shined through with Tubby and his mixing board.

His MCI board was modified to include an Altec high-pass filter now known as Tubby's 'Big Knob' filter. This knob allowed for sweeps to be made very easily through the entire board. Before Tubby used this filter in a creative way, it was generally used as a set and forget control to control the sound instead of change or manipulate it. Veal quotes Prince Jammy saying:

> It was a very unique board because it was custom built for Dynamic Sounds [...] it had things that the modern boards nowadays don't really have, like a high-pass filter that made some squawky sounds when you change the frequency [...] We would put any instrument through it – drums, bass, riddim, voices. That high-pass filter is what create (sic) the unique sound at Tubby's.
> (2007: 114)

This continued with the use of delay and reverb units, but the main focus was on how these all came together in the mixing board.

With the mixing board, Tubby created new ways of hearing and listening to the track. By reconstructing the song, he changed the way that the culture listened to the music. According to Don Ihde (2007): 'In listening humankind belongs within the event. And as a presence, the sound is that which *endures*, which *brought to* pass, the sound *whiles away* in the temporal presecencing that is essential to it'

(261, emphasis added). Tubby shaped the way that the listener heard the music and controlled the events that happened with each track.

The insertion of non-musical sounds became a distinct part of the original dub tracks. Listening for what the engineer had inserted into the space of the track became a focal point for the audience. This allowed for the structure of the track to take precedence over the song itself. Therefore, the way that the track enveloped the listener dominated the listening experience. On 'Skanking Dub' B5, you can hear the space that is created when the original track 'Swing Easy' is manipulated and put through a delay and filters. This song is just one example of the way Tubby created space to envelope the listener. When listening to dub, the space that is formed and what is done in that space become more important than the original track.

Belonging in the event of the soundprint is the point of dub and is what led to the formation of the culture. To be a part of the soundprint/song in a way that utilises hearing to create feeling is what King Tubby designed into his tracks. The ways in which the pre-existing sound was shifted and changed allowed for this to occur. Again, the creative elements that were added and used throughout the mix became the dub and allowed the belonging to happen. While other engineers were adding and removing instruments in their dubs, Tubby was changing every track and processing each one differently to create a soundprint that varied significantly from the original. With his apprentices, he created the dub genre of reggae.

The dub genre begins here as King Tubby and his studio framed the engineer as a musician and artist at the control of a mixing board and other elements in the small studio. This is not dub for just monetary gain, this is creating music through the use of the mixing board. Williams (2012) states: 'This is something more than an engineer carrying out a technical exercise at a mixing desk – it is clearly a highly skilled musician performing with a musical instrument' (251). The faders became the instrument, and how they were manipulated in real time created the sound of King Tubbys and dub music.

Social 5

The use of the mixing board and the creation of dub tracks reflect the surrounding culture of the time and creates a culture based on sound. The sound of dub begins with Tubby's use of the mixing board and what happened in this small home studio. Ihde (2007) states:

> The production of the recorded music lies behind and is presupposed by the end result. The studio is a complex location and process here involved. Acoustical space is constructed; takes, retakes, and increasing musical editing goes into the development of the record such that a simple live-performance recording becomes but one possibility out of many.
>
> (261)

These possibilities were expanded at King Tubbys by him and the many other engineers that worked there.

Tubby's work added another layer to this complexity by taking the constructed space and editing of the original track and rebuilding it entirely. In many of the tracks, the main melody is reconstructed and manipulated completely, in some parts removing Augustus Pablo from the track. This removed the producer of the music and fixated the listener on what the engineer did instead of the producer. While Pablo produced amazing tracks for this record at Randy's, what Tubby did to them was what made this record famous. The possibilities that were opened for the dance hall allowed the culture of dub to spread throughout the world.

Dub is an attempt to create a tone of being lost in thought and centred in space. The enveloping nature of the reverb and the use of non-musical effects creates a feeling of being lost in the music. All of these effects attune the listener to specific feelings of experience. The mood is set by the track and what the engineer has done to it. The song is attempting to produce a scene of contemplation and reflection on basic forms of being.

The dub becomes sonic in ways that envelop and connect the listener to the song. This connection is created through the characteristics that have been mentioned. In 'Sonic dominance and the reggae sound system session', Julian Henriques (2003) situates the sound of reggae and dub through the use of Merleau-Ponty. 'The sonic operates with the qualities of mood, color, texture, timbre and affect, rather than the quantities of measured qualification. The particular spatiality attaching to the sonic has been described as "acoustic space"' (Henriques 2003: 459). This sonic force that dub creates is done through the removal and rebuilding of the track. Through the forms of dub, the space is created.

To discuss space, it is important to attempt to figure out the way the term is being used. In this discussion, space is set up to reflect the emptiness that is created in the music, but it is also discussed as tone in the area between aesthetic experience and named affect. In the case of dub music, the space of the song also contains elements that make the listener think of outer space. This last point does not occur often in other forms of music but is one of the main characteristics of dub. Space, in the first two instances, occurs in many other forms of music. It is this space that allows the music to make the listener 'feel'. Dub utilises space in all three of these ways.

The first instance of space is as an emptiness. How do you create emptiness with music? Listening to a dub track, there is always a suggested melody. Maybe it is established at first and then removed or maybe it is only stated for half of a measure. You can hear this on '555 Dub Street' A5. By setting the tone and then removing elements, this emptiness is left with the listener and within the track. The argument here is that the space belongs to the track. The engineer processing the music creates this space and brings it out in the mix.

The formal characteristics of dub set up a relationship between space and tone. The audience is attuned to this relationship. This description can vary but for many the feeling of ease, zoning out and escape from society become common responses to listening to dub. Part of this re-production is the addition of non-musical sounds and expanded delays and reverb to create the feeling of outer space. This is the third instance of space and relates predominately to dub music. The track is changed and, often literally, expanded from the original and creates a feeling of being in outer space. A sense of floating comes through because of this use of space. Without the re-production of space and sonic dissonance, this effective amplification would not occur.

With the re-production of a song into the reimagined dub version, the listener gets to experience the original melody, only briefly, to feel connected to the song and then can float with the music away from the reality of the surrounding world. The drive towards space and, what is heard in that space, is more pressing than the reality of the original song. The simple, oftentimes homemade, technologies utilised to create the dub version linked the production of the track to the streets and the surrounding society of the time. The feeling of getting lost in a trance is often suggested by listeners, and the focus on the droning bass and drums of the song leads to the feeling of escape.

Through access to the technology of the mixing board and tape machines, Tubby gained a way to construct the world around him through sound. The fact that he was an electrician and repairman before getting into recording cannot be downplayed in his work, as his sound manipulated and changed electronic devices. For many musicians, this is of extreme importance. In 'The problem with music', Steve Albini states: 'Producers who aren't also engineers, and as such, don't have the slightest fucking idea what they're doing in a studio, besides talking all the time' (2018: n.pag.). The person behind the mixing board having knowledge of the engineering principles that are being used establishes a better sound. The ways in which Tubby used what he had reflects the Jamaican experience suggested by others as well. Creating a vocal booth in a bathroom and using a hand me down mixing board to create are just the start of Ruddock's creativity. His dubplates and versions fall into the dub genre of reggae and his creations with the MCI board fall into the version genre, thus spanning the entirety of dub music.

With the growth in recording technologies, Tubby was able to create different ways of listening to tracks. Ihde (2007) suggests:

> For example, once recording technologies were invented, different variations on human-technology relations were introduced. With recording, the live performance while 'casual' in the recording chain of events, once recorded recedes in experienced space-time. Then, with the capacity to manipulate the final result through studio-editing processes, a different set of roles for human actors enters the musical production.
>
> (263)

He is commenting on the overall effect that the studio has on sound and music. By the time that Tubby got behind the mixing board, the possibilities were endless to his creative mind. The original recording became a template to destroy and rebuild with different self-made effects. These effects were heard live in the sound system and became immensely popular.

Tubby's Hometown Hi-Fi became the most popular sound system of the day because it was the best sounding due to Tubby's knowledge of the equipment. Dennis Alcapone tells Lloyd Bradley (2001), '"King Tubby had a sound system that I never hear nothing like in my whole life. Sound Systems, the big ones, was always exciting, but when Tubby came on the scene it was *extraordinary*"' (314, emphasis added). This led to him taking a place within Jamaican popular music that expanded throughout the world. David Hendley (2003) in 'King Tubby', adds:

> Tubby's Hometown Hi-Fi became the first sound to introduce revolutionary innovations such as reverb (echo effects followed later in the early 1970s) built into the amplifiers. He loved to make his chrome fronted amps look as attractive as possible with lights that would flicker in time to the rhythm – at dances people stood around the control area just to admire them.
>
> (n.pag.)

This is just one example of the thought that went behind the music with Tubby. Making lights flash in time with the music being played may seem simple with today's technology, but this was in the early 1970s. You had to be extremely knowledgeable with electronic technology to figure this out, and this was in addition to the music that was being created and played through the self-built sound system.

His first single in 1974 was released in England and started the influence of dub music there and throughout the world. In Erik Davis's work '"Roots and Wires" remix: Polyrhythmic tricks the black electronic', he states,

> dub subtly called it into question by dematerializing and eroding the integrity of singers and song. [...] Dub's analog doppelgangers, spectral distortions, and vocal ghosts produced an imaginal space no less compelling in its own way than the virtual African Zion that organized so much of reggae's Rastafarian longings.
>
> (2008: 63)

Here the space that is created by dub is linked to the Rastafarian movement. Davis connects these two concepts and suggests that this space, and removal of voices, is just as important as the lion that represents Rastafarianism. This also connects to the concept of the community and culture surrounding King Tubbys.

Tubby's Hometown Hi-Fi was also the place to hear the most popular DJs of the time who were always ready to voice something over King Tubby's dubs. In 'King Tubby, the sound creator', Brain

Bonitto (2012) states: 'Deejays U-Roy and Dennis Alcapone were staples on the 'sound' (n.pag.). These DJs influenced the ways that the dubs were utilised and the ways that Tubby created them. Through working back and forth within the sound system, Tubby was able to know exactly what the audience wanted and how to create dubs that allowed the DJ to flow well.

This was a community of singers and musicians coming to the studio to play over the existing track. Tubbys became the place to go for voicings and specials as well as the latest dub tracks. If you were playing on a song from Tubbys, you gained status within the community. This was not due to the bands that were on the song or who played what instrument, this was due to Tubby mixing and distorting the original track and then mixing the vocalist or musician onto that track. The dub was created by doing this, and it opened up the market for many different artists. Rupie Edwards states to Lloyd Bradley (2001):

> When you have the musicians that can play properly, and the correct production and sound balance and the recording was done real well, then of course you can version it again and again. As long as it's balanced: drum, bass, guitar [...] everything. With those songs all the ingredients was always there, not like so many modern songs where it isn't cooked properly so it can't last long.
>
> (333)

Through the manipulation of the mixing board, Tubby was able to create a culture surrounding his house and studio.

Another important element that occurred at King Tubby's studio was how the music was already recorded prior to being brought into the studio. The existing tracks for *King Tubby Meets the Rockers Uptown* were all recorded at Randy's studio and produced by Augustus Pablo. Having these existing tracks, played by outstanding musicians, Tubby was able to control and manipulate music that was already excellent. Many of the songs that appear on the album were previously hits or popular in the dance hall, and this allowed for an ease of manipulation. As stated by Edwards above, the most important part of a dub is the original tracks being recorded flawlessly.

The studio was in the Waterhouse area of Kingston, which was a part of St Andrew and a tough inner-city area. If you had a voice or an instrument that was needed for the mix, then you would be invited to record. Tubby gained many followers and apprentices with the best-known ones, Lloyd 'King Jammy's' James and Hopeton 'Scientist' Brown, going on to their own large success. In the 1980s, Tubby built a larger studio and started the Firehouse, Waterhouse, and Taurus labels. These labels released songs by Anthony Red Rose, Sugar Minott, Conroy Smith and others. 'The Firehouse Crew, which went on to record and tour with Luciano and Sizzla, started out at Tubby's Waterhouse studio' (Anon. 2008: n.pag.). David Katz (2015) adds: 'Nevertheless, the remix culture we take for granted today is largely reliant on Tubby's ingenuity, the techniques he introduced indelibly changing the way contemporary popular music is made and issued' (n.pag.). The Jamaican underground eventually caught up to King Tubby, but it was due to money and not politics. On February 6, 1989, King Tubby was murdered by a gunman, in an attempted robbery, outside of his house at 85 Sherwood Crescent in Dunhaney park. The murder has not been solved as one of the greatest influencers of music died.

Timbre 6

The album opens with a statement of 'Lion' and A1 'Keep on Dubbing'. Tubby plays with the music while pushing the bass up through the mix. The horn melody begins the song and the piano hits hard in the mix, and then the bass line is made prominent. The interesting thing about the opening track is the way that the melody comes in and out of the bass line. This is a dub of Jacob Miller's 'Keep on Knocking', and the re-production of the track is where Tubby displays his creativity and force. As the track progresses, the bass stays at a consistent level while the other elements are brought in and out of the mix and panned from the left to right channel. After establishing the identity of the song, the track dissolves into the basic rhythm in the bass and drums with occasional hits from the piano and guitar. The guitar and piano are delayed and continue to sound after the initial hit. This blends the sound of the piano and guitar into the rhythm of the track. Tubby brings the horns back with small hits and decays the horn tone through more delay. The drums continue to remain in the background aside from an occasional hit that has been processed through a tape delay. The track is 3:11 long, but the space created makes the track seem much longer. This occurs throughout the album, and the first track grounds the record in the bass timbre that is heard throughout dub.

In A2 'Stop Them Jah', the horn line brings the song in as well and then disappears for the bass to take the lead. The way in which the horns are processed through the delay and high-pass filter is interesting here as well. By putting the horns through these filters, the high-pitched nature of the horns is removed, and the darker tones come through. The bass drives this track as well, and the overall tone of the song is dark and brooding. The track is a mix of Jacob Miller's 'Who Say Jah No Dread' and Hugh Mundell's 'Stop them Jah' but is in a different key and removes the melodica from the original with Augustus Pablo. By taking the original track and manipulating the key, the song becomes dark and the timbre shifts.

Rhythmic interplay 6
On A3 'Young Generation Dub', the tone is a bit brighter as the horns are kept in the mix. The rhythmic interplay here is shown in the upbeats of the horns. The original track is by Bongo Pat and called 'Young Generation'. The vocals on the original track are classic and the melodica line, played by Pablo adds an ethereal feel to the track. The guitar and piano have been stripped in the track and the horns carry the song with the bass and drums. The horns are still panned from left and right in a sweeping motion and processed through a delay that keeps them darker sounding. The way that the bass and drums are used here frames the song, and while the horns are loud in the mix, the bass line drives the track and is the loudest throughout the song.

Instead of using the guitars and piano for rhythmic interplay in this track, the horns are used on the upbeats in between the main melody line. While the bass line is important here, how Tubby used the horns is the key to this track. The manipulation of the drum track also takes place heavily throughout the song and towards the end of the track, it is almost destroyed by effects letting the horns fade away.

A4 'Each One Dub' is back to dubbing a Jacob Miller tune called 'Each One Teach One' and takes the original vocal and chops and distorts it. Here, the piano and guitar come in loudly to display the rhythmic interplay of the original song. They are mixed with cuts of the vocal line and used to propel the track. The bass and drums are loudest here, and there are multiple occurrences of the drums being manipulated. You can hear the resonance of the bleed-through from the vocal line throughout the track as the bass rolls over the entire thing.

Re-production 6
The focus of this entire album is in the re-production of each track. King Tubby differentiated himself and his studio through the ways in which these songs were constructed and manipulated. The songs all sound like they belong to a more contemporary world where mixing and producing are 'easy' through computer-aided systems. While listening to this album, the listener consistently hears newer sounds and techniques of re-production that are still being used today.

A5 '555 Dub Street' demonstrates this re-production first by stripping the original Jacob Miller track 'False Rasta' of the melodica and vocals. The track then builds on the high hat of the drum and the bass line. With each addition of the piano and melodica, the delay and high pass filter are used. The 'Big Knob' here is used on every track, including the drums and the sounds pan from left to right channel as they sweep along in the mix. There are delayed hits and trills of the melodica that create a spacey vibe to the track as the high hat keeps the time. The timbre of the bass stays consistent as the other elements come in and out of the mix. The A-side closes with one of the most creative tracks of dub ever originally produced.

The B-side opens with B1 'Brace Tower Dub', a dub of Dillinger's 'Brace a Boy'. Starting off with a drum fill into a piano rhythmic interplay with no bass at all, the track then flows with the drums and bass, while the piano accents the melody line and the guitar is modified to add to the rhythmic interplay. Again, the re-production here resonates throughout the track as Tubby creates space with the filter and delay unit that was completely innovative. The removal of the vocal is the easy item in this mix, and the dere-production and rebuild is the point. Tubby cuts everything out in the mix in time and then brings them back. He remakes the main song into an almost completely different track as the sounds are manipulated throughout. The only thing left of the original is the piano.

B2 'King Tubby Meets Rockers Uptown' is the lead single off the album and is a dub of Jacob Miller's 'Baby I Love You So'.

The original melodica and vocal intro are in the track, and then it dissolves into another example of Tubby's constructive genius. The track rides on the high hat and bass line to give it an aggressive feel that is not in the original sweet love song. The delayed hits from the guitar and piano are also used to push the track, and the sweeps of the 'Big Knob' are heard here as well. The way that Tubby brings the vocal in at certain times also creates a warm eerie feel that would become synonymous with dub from here on out. This song was released in 1974 as a 45-rpm single by Mango records with the Jacob Miller song on the B-side. It is this track that led to the spread of dub to England and throughout the world, influencing Johnny Rotten and others.

B3 'Corner Crew Dub' takes another Hugh Mundell song 'One Jah, One Aim, One Destiny' and deconstructs it to rebuild a new song. The melodica is the most important element here in the re-production as it is delayed and processed multiple times in the track. The original track has much more rhythmic interplay from the melodica. By removing this, the space allows for additions of melodica runs and flare. The piano runs are in the original, but Pablo plays runs throughout this dub that mimic the piano and that Tubby pushes through the effects. The bass line is also manipulated so that it pulls out of tune in places, and this allows the timbre to be a bit higher than the other tracks on this album but still rooted in the bass line. This also creates a constructive element that is not heard on the record before this, as the original bass line is high pitched, Tubby creates the song's timbre around it and the melodica.

In B4 'Say So', Tubby constructs the original song 'Say So' by Paul Black man aka Paul Whiteman and again creates a dark tone by removing the lead vocal and focusing on the bass and drums. He processes the original guitar through a spring reverb, and this effect is boosted in volume on the dub. The delay is used on the drum hits as the guitar and piano swell in different parts of the song. The original rhythmic interplay comes in and out but is manipulated with the delay, and the backing vocals are removed but briefly come in towards the end of the track. This is another example of the re-production that went into each track of this album. The vocal 'Say so' is only heard twice in the track to reference the original, but the bass line remains consistent grounding the song in a dark tone.

B5 'Skanking Dub' takes one of the most popular songs of the day, 'Swing Easy' by the Soul Vendors, and dubs a version that Augustus Pablo had done called 'Skanking Easy'. The familiarity of the track is almost deconstructed out of it as Tubby puts everything through a filter and delay. The melodica comes in and hints at the melody and the bass line is here, but the re-production of the drums and the swirl of the high hat are prominent here. In 'Skanking Easy', Pablo plays the lead on the melodica and slows the song down to a reggae groove. Here Tubby takes that track and constructs a sweeping version with only glimpses on Pablo's lead line. Even this is delayed and processed to add space and depth to the melodica line. This track shows the reuse of the same song from two different producers and engineers and demonstrates what can be done with a high-pass filter and delay.

The Heptones' song 'Love Won't Come Easy' gets Tubby's treatment in B6 'Frozen Dub'. A sweet love song with the amazing harmonies of the Heptones gets slowed down and constructed as another darker dub track. The volume is played with as Pablo plays melodica over the original tracks. The melodica line is then delayed as the dub focuses on the bass line pushed so hard in the mix that it distorts in places. The drums propel the song and are given a similar treatment of being processed through certain parts of the song. Even the bridge to this track is completely distorted as the entire songs goes through a dissolution. The lyrics do not come into the track at all, and the only resonance of the melody is kept in the piano. This allows for the love song about mom telling you that love will not come easily to become a dark, spacey and bass resonant track.

The last track B7 'Satta Dub' is an unlisted track on the original release and is a dub of the Abyssinian's 'Satta Massagana' that was recorded at Lee Perry's Black Ark studio. The original track was another popular song in the dance halls, and Tubby reconstructs it into a dark, syncopated, spaced out track. The song is slowed down, and the horns are replaced with Pablo's melodica. The original vocals are removed, and the rhythmic interplay of the piano and guitar are at the beginning of the track but quickly removed. There is an added percussion hit of a vibraslap, shakers and other percussion that add to the rhythmic interplay as the bass drives the song. The re-production here is the focus and what Tubby did to the track is what is interesting about the song.

Completion 5

With the re-production of a song into the reimagined dub version, the listener gets to experience the original melody, only briefly, to feel connected to the song and then can float with the music away from the reality of the surrounding world. The drive towards space, and what is heard in that space, is more pressing than the reality of the original song. The simple, oftentimes homemade, technologies utilised to create the dub version linked the production of the track to the streets and the surrounding society of the time. The feeling of getting lost in a trance is often suggested by listeners, and the focus on the droning bass and drums of the song leads to the feeling of escape.

The formal characteristics of dub are central to the creation of space in the track. Through the re-production of the track, the engineer reforms the song with a different tone. The use of space in three different ways sets the listener into a feeling of escape and removal from the harshness of society. The actual space of the track through the removal of parts allows for the insertion of non-musical effects that focus the audience on the insertions instead of the music. This allows for the connection to the track in different ways than the original mix.

The soundprint of the engineer can be heard, and the connection to the event takes place within this space. With the use of the studio, the engineer became a musician with the mixing board as an instrument. King Tubby was one of the first to utilise the mixing board in such a creative way and created dub culture by doing so.

King Tubbys Meets Rockers Uptown demonstrated what could be done in the studio, with a creative genius behind the mixing board. The manipulations of the technology are the main reasons that this album is so important to music. Not only did this record start the culture of dub, but it also spread dub throughout the world because of its quality. There were many other engineers dubbing music, for both monetary gain and creative purposes, but King Tubby was the most creative and innovative of them all. The music that came out of a front room studio crossed over version and dub genres and became, what most people, call dub. In *Bass Culture*, Lloyd Bradley states:

> His uncanny ability to get inside a song and, as he stripped away the layers, expose its heart produced some of the best roots music to come out of Jamaica. Militant, conscious, righteous, praising

> Jah Rastafari, lovers' rock [...] it didn't matter; King Tubby would get to grips with everything.
>
> (2001: 322)

Island Records UK planned to release Jacob Miller's 'Baby I Love You So' on the A-side with 'King Tubbys Meets Rockers Uptown' on the B-side as the dub but someone suggested to flip the sides and dub was released to the rest of the world. 'This wasn't the engineer as artist, this was the engineer as rock god' (Bradley 2001: 324). After this release, dub and dub culture began to spread throughout England and to the rest of the world. The importance of the track being reused and manipulated became central to what a dub was and the version genre that had originally begun dub fell into the background. The self-created effects that King Tubby had used and, the way that he manipulated each track, became signatures in dub and dub culture.

Chapter 6
The New Sound: England and the Spread of Culture

The analogue thing of dub makes the sound leak out of the speaker.
                                            Adrian Sherwood (2019)

As the music of dub travelled to England, the culture developed alongside it. Mixing British youth subculture and Jamaican street culture, the people began to immerse themselves in dub. The development of Rock Against Racism spurred the mix of culture through performance and political action and the bands that were a part of it propelled the music into the mainstream. What began as the Two-Tone movement with ska taking over the charts, led to more fans discovering dub and making it their own. There are many strains of music that developed out of the original dub albums that were played including drum and bass, breakbeat, jungle and grime, all of which continue to be popular styles of dance music in the United Kingdom and around the world. This all began when dub was played on the radio by Johnny Rotten and taken forward by those who heard it. Groups like the Cimarons, Aswad, Steel Pulse and Matumbi were all taking the music that they heard and had brought with them to a new level in production. Combining newer recording equipment with the traditional sounds created a different and British sound. This all began with the immigration that occurred from the Caribbean after World War II.

Arriving on the *MV Empire Windrush* cruise ship in Tilbury on 22 June 1948, people from Jamaica, Trinidad and Tobago, and other Caribbean islands came to England to fill shortages in labor. The first 492 or so immigrants, many of whom were children, came to England with the hope of attaining work and sending money back to their home countries. This was the Windrush generation, and many others followed up to 1971 when the immigration act put a halt to the arrivals as it became more difficult to become a British citizen. This generation became central to the development of reggae, dub and other forms of Jamaican and Caribbean music throughout England.

David Matthews' (2018) book *Voices of the Windrush Generation: The Real Story Told by the People Themselves* contains many excellent stories from this important generation of people. He also starts the book off by stating: 'Coming from an arbitrary world of smash and grab colonialism, the Windrush generation knew the importance of having an identity, figuratively and literally' (Matthews 2018: 7). It was this collective 'identity' that would go on to begin and support, the rise of Jamaican music in England.

The people of the Windrush generation and their children were influential in the development of sound system parties and creating the Notting Hill carnival. This event draws millions of people every year to the Notting Hill area of London and celebrates Caribbean culture. The sounds and parties that surround this event began with the small dances that were held by the members of this generation. '"Windrushers" as they are now affectionately known, have transmogrified into something akin to a British institution' (Matthews 2018: 257). It is this first wave of Jamaican and Caribbean immigrants that began the distillation of sound in England.

Dub in England was received much differently than in Jamaica. In England, dub was for house parties and afterhours places in the university and other areas. The bass rumbled through the speakers and allowed for the youth to attempt to gain an understanding of what they considered Jamaican music. Many people have written about dub in England as a foundation or roots music, and this is true, but it also becomes even more rooted in class politics as it comes to the United Kingdom. Jamaican dub was often viewed as a version of the original track with little modification and a focus on the DJ or singer voicing a new sound. When dub gets to England, it starts to shift to actual performances of songs and recordings being produced specifically to and for dubbing.

One of the first dub records to come out in the United Kingdom was *Natty Locks Dub* by Winston Edwards in 1974. This record was mixed in Jamaica at King Tubby's and was recorded at Black Ark and Joe Gibbs's studio. Edwards would go on to work with Dennis Bovell on one of the most important dub records to be released in England, *Dub Conference: Winston Edwards & Blackbeard at 10 Downing Street* in 1980. Edwards would also release other great dub albums that were mostly engineered and recorded in Jamaica. The transfer between England and the United Kingdom in dub begins here.

Dub Conference is somewhat problematic in that it is a producer's album with little regard for the writer and musicians. Dennis Bovell stated that the record should never have come out and that it was created from tracks that were made in the studio and then left there. Bovell (2019) states: 'Actually, those dub mixes were done as a favor to Winston Edwards. They were never done with the intention of releasing an album'. Edwards and Winston Mathews, as producer, put the record out without confirmation from Bovell or the Wellpack band who had performed on it. The record is still a classic and one that is coveted by many fans of dub, but the way that it appeared is a typical story of the record industry in the late 1970s and 1980s.

The studio band consisted of Jah Bunny on drums, John Kpiaye on guitar, Bovell on bass and Noel Salmon on keyboard. This band, supporting the vocal trio called Brown Sugar, recorded 'Our Reggae Music' in 1977 and many other songs that they never received full credit or compensation for, even though this song and two others topped the charts in England and became standards in the genre known as Lover's Rock.

The other record that is often stated as the first dub record in the United Kingdom is Keith Hudson's *Pick a Dub* in 1974. Adrian Sherwood (2019) was influenced in his work by Hudson and Prince Far-I, who he worked closely with and said about Hudson: 'He was a man who prided himself on having a really slow one drop and having loads of space in sound'. This change in speed and emptiness of the track became signature sounds for Sherwood's On-U Sound record label. Hudson's 1974 release *Pick a Dub* defined a new take on dub with a slower, even more, laid back and empty style. There is a definitive removal of sounds in each track that allows the song to float as it plays. This was Hudson's style.

Pick a Dub was on the Mamba/Atra label. The record contains remixes of famous riddims, such as 'Satta Massagana' and a melodica track from Augustus Pablo. The fader moves throughout this record create so much space in the mix that, at times, the song is completely emptied of sound. The record is a complete dub album as it reuses previously existing tracks to create something new that was influenced by the engineer. This is a classic example of the dub genre in reggae, as discussed previously, and sits with the other examples of an intended complete dub album.

The sound that occurred in the United Kingdom differed in production technique but not in playing style and form. The original UK groups were all very seasoned musicians that knew the music well and framed the songs in ways that reflected the politics of the United Kingdom. The Cimarons were the first reggae group to emigrate from Jamaica to England in the mid-1970s and then in 1978 Island Records released *Handsworth Revolution* by Steel Pulse with the single 'Ku Klux Klan' featured on it. The title referenced the Handsworth area of Birmingham, England, and reached #9 on the British music charts only 10 days after its release. The group then went on a tour opening for Bob Marley & the Wailers in 1978 becoming the lead reggae band of the United Kingdom. The album was produced by Karl Pitterson who had worked with Marley, Peter Tosh and many others from Jamaica for Island Records.

Migrating to England in 1967, the Cimarons were the first reggae group in England. They had been a backing and studio band previously in Jamaica and came to England to release *In Time* on Trojan Records in 1974. Their major tour in support of Sham 69 broke them into the punk community and the youth culture of the day. The group consisted of Franklyn Dunn on bass, Carl Levy on keyboards, Locksley Gichie on guitar, Maurice Ellis on drums and Winston Reedy as a vocalist.

The Cimarons released 'On the Rock' in 1976 on Vulcan records that did not chart well. This record and single, along with touring with Sham 69, garnered them many fans, but they remained in the underground and as studio musicians. This tour would see one of the first times that black and white musicians were on the same stage in England. Reggae's crossover to the traditional skinhead movement begins with this band. They backed Jimmy Cliff in the studio and were the go-to studio band for many Jamaican artists coming to England. Their stage presence and choices of covers left many purists upset with the group, but they continued to play and produce songs that began reggae in the United Kingdom. Their album *Maka*, released on Ploydor in 1978, would be their most respected work as they wrote the album themselves. The Cimarons started the path for many other groups to emerge that were specifically British in the reggae that they played.

Steel Pulse consisted of David Hinds, vocals, Basil Gabbidon, vocals and lead guitar, Alphonso Martin and Mykaell Riley, vocals and percussion, Ronald McQueen, bass and vocals, Selwyn Brown, keyboards and vocals and Steve Nisbett, drums, for this record. The focal point of the sound lies in the vocal harmonies over the rhythm. Karl Pitterson began his career in Jamaica as a house engineer at Dynamics, Federal, Randy's, Studio One, Treasure Isle and Aquarius. Being schooled in the Jamaican reggae tradition of recording led to this album becoming steeped in the sound of Jamaica.

The group still performs and is led by David Hinds. Their newest release, *Mass Manipulation*, continues their fight against the tyranny of the world and was nominated for a Grammy Award in 2019. From their updated website: 'In the midst of today's strife and turmoil, *Mass Manipulation* is Steel Pulse's indispensable musical gift, as their forty-year legacy continues to define the magnificent power and beauty of reggae music' (Steel Pulse 2019: n.pag.). From their start, Steel Pulse continues to uphold the same message and dedication to writing and performing music that resonates within the political world.

Handsworth Revolution would also be the first time that many people in the United Kingdom heard a specifically British form of Jamaican music. Steel Pulse represented the immigration of the Jamaican people to England through their sound and lyrics. They also represented the working-class people of England, and this combination led to chart success and a cultural shift within the music. On 30 April 1978, an estimated 80,000 people marched from Trafalgar square to Hackney against the mounting racism in England at the time. This march ended with a performance by the Clash, X-ray Spex and Steel Pulse. This was the culmination of the Rock Against Racism campaign, which was formed in reaction to Eric Clapton's on-stage speech on 5 August 1976.

Reggae and dub from that point on represented the fight against the mounting racism of the National Front in England.

In *Walls Come Tumbling Down*, Daniel Rachel (2016) states: 'Through music, and a general sense of disenfranchisement, both first-generation black British and dis-affected white youth – often educated in integrated schools and socializing in the same pubs and clubs-began to recognize common grievances' (xxi).

The music of reggae led the charge and the first Rock Against Racism concert was held with Carol Grimes, Matumbi and Limousine performing on 10 December 1977. In Rachel's book, Dennis Bovell stated: 'I met Red in a pub in New Cross and he had this idea for black and white bands to play on the same stage. So, over a few pints, I said "Yeah, Matumbi will do it"' (cited in Rachel 2016: 18). From this beginning, Rock Against Racism developed into a force in the underground community.

Dennis Bovell was the pioneer of dub in England and the United Kingdom. His band Matumbi was legendary at creating a sound that was distinct. According to Phillip Williams (2018) in '10 essential UK reggae and dub albums', Bovell mixed Adrian Sherwood's first record and told him: 'You go in the studio, record all these great musicians and great performers. And when you go in the studio to make the mix, now that's your time to express yourself' (n.pag.). The focus here is on the initial tracks that were used for the mix. As previously stated by others, the musicianship on the tracks and the quality of them dictated the dub and the ease of manipulation.

As the 1970s closed and the 1980s began, the technology grew immensely. There were many electronic inventions that influenced the studios in England and the rest of the world. Bovell states that they came across a Mellotron in RG Jones studio that was left there by Brian Jones. This board allowed Bovell to capture and manipulate new sounds. These new technologies offered the engineer even more room and space to play with and within the mix.

Bovell began his studio work at Goosebury studios in London at 19 Gerrard st, Soho. Projects with the 4th Street Orchestra, Matumbi and Linton Kwesi Johnson all were completed here, and the genre known as Lover's rock is said to have started here with Bovell at the helm. His preferred mixing board, at the time, was the MCI board. He tells the story:

> What happened was, that Jon Anderson of Yes had bought one
> and left it in London with an engineer friend who worked at a place

called AdVision. His name was Mike and he had custody of this recording equipment while John was away on tour. So, some friends inveigled him to take it to a farm (Ridge Farm Studios) and set it up. I think Roxy Music did their first recording in there. And then after that, I went in there with a group called the Pop Group, then another group called the Slits. Then I did a Matumbi album there and a Marie Pierre album.

(Bovell 2019)

After the MCI board, Bovell used Soundcraft boards to record and used a 16/24 for his recordings and started to do his own solo stuff. He also ran Jah Sufferer sound system and played and produced many dubplates for sound systems around the United Kingdom. In Tim Cumming's article in *Independent,* 'Dennis Bovell: The dub master' Bovell states: 'Dub was just coming up in a big way, and I knew how to do it' (2006: n.pag.).

He formed Matumbi in the late 1960s and had a hit song in 1976 with 'After Tonight' and then again in 1979 reaching the UK Top 10 with 'The Man in Me'. He also released one of the first dub albums in the United Kingdom. *Strictly Dub Wize* in 1978 as Blackbeard, on the Tempus label. *I Wah Dub* was released in 1980 on More Cut/EMI and helped to spur the dub movement in England. He went on to produce works by Fela Kuti, Alpha Blondy, the Slits and even Bananarama.

> Dub is free. You can't schedule it. You can stop or refuse to stop at any time, hang onto one chord for as long as you like. The song falls through a mineshaft, then you go back to it, and it's great to whip up that different feeling. As long as you get out of it where you came in.
>
> (Cumming 2006: n.pag.)

At RG Jones studio in London, Bovell cut dubplates on Saturday mornings. Bovell states: 'The guy who owned it, old Mr. Jones, he would let me come in on a Saturday morning to cut acetates. I got to know about that through a guy called Hot Rod, who worked at Trojan Records' (Bovell 2019). Matumbi's first single, 'Brother Louie (Hot Chocolate)', a cover they did that had Bovell as the singer, was released by Trojan. This song is about an interracial relationship and, in 1973, was a strong statement into the English populace. The single is a great example of the Trojan records' sound of reggae, with the insertion of strings and other production techniques to cross over to the more contemporary market.

Along with Bovell, and his studio, many studios were important in bringing dub to the United Kingdom. One of the most important, at the beginning, was Ariwa studios owned by Neil Joseph Stephen Fraser, aka Mad Professor.

Ariwa was a key element in the beginning of dub and other forms of reggae in England. Opening in 1979 in the front room of 19 Bruce Road, Thornton Heath, South London, Ariwa began as a small setup, but with the critical ear of Fraser, the tracks soon began to resonate, and the studio grew. Fraser began like many of the Jamaican engineers, as an actual electrical engineer building and repairing radios and mixing boards. In 'The Ariwa/Mad Professor story', Fraser tells Katz:

> I analysed the records, like King Tubby's records, analysed them and found out what they're doing and tried to emulate them. I was an electronic technician, started to work for places like Reddifon Rediffusion; I was gifted in that, so I didn't have to study it, I just read books, maybe not learning it the proper way but I learn it my way, just learned electronics and sound engineering. Soundcraft had this job going and I went and the guy showed me a big pile of boards that was thrown in a corner; he said, "These boards got faults" and nobody could fix them – he said, "I'll give you two days trying, if you could fix them then you've got a job" and I managed to fix all the boards, so I stayed there for two years until I started professionally with the studio.
>
> (2018: n.pag.)

From this beginning, Mad Professor grew his studio from a 4-track, to 8, then a 16-track recording local musicians and gaining a foothold in the scene. The dub that started it all was 'Kunte Kinte' by Brixton-based band Aquizim. Moving to the basement of 42 Gautrey rd in Peckham in 1982 saw the growth of technology for the studio with an Ampex MM1000 tape machine, to an ACES 16 track machine, and finally to an Ampex 1100 24 track machine that was gotten from Virgin studios called the Barge. The first of the *Dub Me Crazy* series came out in 1982, after many successes with lover's rock records. By 1993, the series was up to chapter 12 and followed with the *Black*

Liberation Dub series. He worked and toured with Lee 'Scratch' Perry during this time and had a long-standing relationship of recording and creating music together with him.

Fraser often discusses dub as Jamaican producers' answers to American producers' work. Because of the radio signal from America to Jamaica, the music came through slightly off time or sounding a bit different to the people of Jamaica. These early records, even when the format of records changed from 78 to 45 rpm changed the way that the people heard the music. He stated that the B-side of a James Brown record was influential to him as he began listening to music and recording. These influences carried him into his career as one of the most influential contemporary engineers in dub (Fraser 2018).

Mad Professor still continues to make music and collaborates with contemporary artists like Jah 9 and many others in the studio's new home at 34 Whitehorse Lane, London. The influence of Mad Professor throughout the world is a distinct one that runs through groups like The Ruts DC, Bim Skala Bim, the Beastie Boys, the Orb, Sade, Massive Attack, Perry Farrell, Jamiroquai and many Japanese, Brazilian and Argentinian artists.

Another key person in dub in the United Kingdom was, and still is, Adrian Sherwood. Starting with a job for the Carib Gems record label as a junior director, he then founded many different labels initially in an attempt to bring together Jamaican artists in England. Doing so successfully in the early 1980s under the moniker of Singers and Players, artists like Prince Far I, Mikey Dread, Bim Sherman and others found a home on Sherwood's On-U Sound label. With this foundation, Sherwood worked with Lee 'Scratch' Perry on the 1986 release *Time Boom X De Devil Dead*.

From there, groups Sherwood put together to record in the studio included Creation Rebel, Dub Syndicate and African Head Charge. These all had a focus of adding something different to the Jamaican sound but remaining true to the roots of the style. This made On-U Sound stand out and gained many followers. Sherwood was also friends with John Lydon. In Gregory Mario Whitfield's 'The Adrian Sherwood interview: The On-U sound experience, the On-U sound family', Sherwood states:

> I can tell you that John Lydon really helped the progress of roots and culture in Britain at that time. It was around that time, not

long after he'd been beaten up here in London that he went on to radio and played Dr Alimantado's *Born for A Purpose*. Alimantado was immediately shot to cult status as a result!
(cited in Whitfield 2003: n.pag.)

The concept of dub as a 'cult status' is extremely important as it arrives in England. The fact that dub was viewed as a music listened to in the underground gave it clout even among the punk scene and its other offshoot sects. The music was championed by Lydon and gave the sound new life through underground parties and in the university areas. The sound of the streets of Jamaica distilled and reformed in England as a sound of the underground.

Sherwood has worked with artists like The Slits, Cabaret Voltaire, Nine Inch Nails, Ministry, The Fall, Sinead O'Connor and many more. Throughout this work, his focus has been on incorporating new or different sounds that are not common to production techniques. He has stated that he was one of the first people in the roots and reggae genre to record a track backwards and add sounds to it so that when it is played forward you hear the music playing backwards. This is just one example of his production style. This, incorporated with the drive to compete and beat the Jamaican groups coming to England to perform, gave On-U sound and his productions their distinct style.

Social 7

The racism in England in the mid-1970s created a huge culture of musicians and artists that rose up against it. Rock Against Racism, created by Red Saunders, gave these musicians a way to perform together in support against the cause. These shows also gave rise to Two-Tone and other movements that were based on fighting racism and fascism. Having black and white musicians perform on stage together was shocking to the British audiences, and many times the black performers were spit at and forced off stage. In Daniel Rachel's *Walls Come Tumbling Down*, Mykaell Riley states:

> Traditionally, promoters didn't promote a mixed gig; you had a black gig, you had a white gig: rock or reggae. You were targeting a different audience. Steel Pulse was the first black band in the UK

Figure 6.1: Dennis Bovell and the author. Photo by author (2018).

to be playing white clubs outside of London on the same bill as punks. That was the interesting synergy because punks understood and identified with what we were doing.

(cited in Rachel 2016: 58)

These performances would inspire Jerry Dammers and many others to use music to spread a message of togetherness and a fight against the National Front. This is where reggae as a political force truly comes into its own. Dub plays a large role in this as John Lydon and others continued to promote the music and champion artists. This relationship became solidified when Lydon had Linton Kwesi Johnson read poetry before a show at the Rainbow and shouted at the audience as they booed Johnson that this was a mate of his. The audience then listened and appreciated the artist.

There is a great deal written on the Rock Against Racism movement and 2-tone records. These two elements in England were the culmination of many artists before them performing in clubs where they were not wanted and dealing with racism in many forms. Bovell (2019) states: 'Lynval (Golding) told me that when he heard Matumbi's "Blue Beat and Ska" he was like, "Yeah we should do a ska band." And then the Specials were born'. Dub became a music that was listened to in the dance clubs and homes of people who supported this cause. In many ways, dub became the underground music of the underground. While reggae and punk were on stage and fighting against racism and fascism, dub was what the DJ spun between bands and what was listened to during the after parties. The production and work in the studio of dub engineers would translate to the anti-racism fight, but it was the reggae and punk bands that were on the front lines.

Rock Against Racism grew into a force that was almost too big to control. With Margaret Thatcher gaining office, the movement was at a point of implosion as it became very large and infighting began. The culmination of the movement happened with a compilation record called *RAR's Greatest Hits*. The force behind this album was Red Saunders and John Dennis. In *Walls Come Tumbling Down*, Dennis states:

> There was Carol Grimes, Stiff Little Fingers, Gang of Four, The Piranhas, Barry Ford Band, X-ray Spex, Matumbi, Steel Pulse, Aswad, TRB doing a live version of "Winter of '79," "Goon Squad" from Elvis Costello, the Mekons, the Cimarons, the Members, and I had three versions of the Clash's "White Man in Hammersmith Palais" to choose from.
>
> (cited in Rachel 2016: 216)

This album would lead to the split of RAR due to the commercialisation of the movement, but the spirit of the movement carried forward and would lead to the Two-Tone label's formation. Without the bands and organisers of RAR, music would not be the same as this was the first time that black and white musicians were seen together on stage in England. Dub was the key musical element that connected these groups together and bridged the differences between punk and reggae.

Dennis Bovell became a key innovator in the bridge between live performance and engineered dub. As a performer with Matumbi, he played a critical role in the first show for Rock

Against Racism and as an engineer and producer put out the first full-length dub albums in the United Kingdom. 'We were propositioned to join forces against evil. I think any person with good intent would join that, because we mustn't let evil overcome good' (Bovell 2019). He was also a critical component in connecting people like John Lydon to Linton Kwesei Johnson and others in the punk community to the reggae community.

Timbre 7

When dub culture came to the United Kingdom, it fractured into many forms and styles. The closest to the original at the beginning was Dennis Bovell's *Strictly Dub Wize* in 1978 under the pseudonym Blackbeard. For this chapter, the focus will be on this album, but the works of Keith Hudson, Mad Professor, Adrian Sherwood and Burning Spear all play large roles in the distillation of sound and dub culture to the United Kingdom. Without all of these producers and groups, dub would not have travelled throughout the world. Written and recorded in 1978 at Goosebury studios and released on Moving Target/Tempus records, this full-length record, *Strictly Dub Wize*, features sounds that were designed by Bovell.

The musicians on the record include Jah Bunny on drums, Euton 'Fergus' Jones on percussion and Bagga Walker on bass. Bovell played keyboard, guitar and some bass on the record while engineering and producing. Dave Hunter is also credited as an engineer for this record. One of the biggest changes that occurred as dub came to the United Kingdom was in the fact that these dub records were written for dubbing. This was not reusing a song to expand its marketability or to make money off an existing song format. This was creating music to be dubbed. This began with Matumbi and Bovell using dub techniques on stage life and spread to the studio.

With this different focus on creation, the album, as a whole, shares the timbre with the original dub records that came before it. What becomes interesting is the way that the mix is handled by Bovell. Being the musician and engineer allowed him to write and perform the music with a strong bass timbre at the starting point. This is very different from an engineer or a producer removing sounds and timbre from songs that were already hits. The tracklist for this album is A1 'Cut After Cut', A2 'Rebel Chase', A3 'Ites of Dub', A4 'River to Bank', A5 'Tell Yuh So', B1 'Strictly Dub', B2 'Mint Ah Music', B3 'Ska Be Doo Za' and B4 'Ah Weh'.

Distillation of Sound

The record opens with A1 'Cut After Cut' and begins with a drum roll and then into the main bass line and groove. This bass line is heavily forward in the mix of the song and creates a ground for the other sounds and instruments to play on. The organ holds in the beginning are also set to a lower timbre than would normally be heard in an organ. After the holds are mixed out of the mix, the bass and drums take over with a drum pattern that is immensely interesting.

The drums on this track are very busy for a standard dub track and have many more hits than other previous dub recordings. It is suggested here that this is due to the fact that the track was written to be dubbed, with the drummer aware that the song was focused on the bass and drum parts with everything else being added sporadically. The snare sound is set very low in the tonal register as well, and the snare pattern is not a standard one drop of reggae but a steppers or heartbeat pattern on the kick drum. With this, the side stick hits of the snare cut through the mix and give the song title its feel. The snare hits literally take the track and cut after cut through it.

This track also uses the delay processor on everything except the bass line giving the rest of the track a wash that envelopes the listener. At 1:15 into the track, the drums are cut to let the cutting stop and the delay and bass carry through. This happens again at 2:10, and throughout the track, this delay becomes extremely important in setting the tone. The way the instruments are processed through this delay sounds like a digital delay was used as well as the timing for the delay is consistent throughout the entire track, keeping the bass mixed more loudly than the washed-out drums and other instruments in the song.

The other interesting tonal element in this track is the high-pitched tambourine that rides through the entire song, aside from the two breaks. This shaking is not processed through a delay but carries the rhythm with the snare and side stick cutting the entire track. The tambourine mimics the high-hat pattern here and ground the rhythm to allow the snare hits to come through. The piano and guitar run that come in and out of the song also add to the interest of the dub.

On A2 'Rebel Chase', the timbre is again established from the beginning by the deep bass line. The difference here is the mainline in the piano that is played from the beginning. This line is played in the lower register of the piano and not affected very much here. It is mixed lower than the bass line, but the piano floats over the riddim throughout the beginning of the track until the organ comes in to match the melody line. The drum pattern here is a standard one drop, and the tonal element that is featured here is the sound of the main melody line on both piano and organ.

These two instruments trading off on the melody line, with various embellishments, demonstrates how a melody line can resonate in the lower tonal register as well. It is not until 2:53 into the track that the piano changes register and finishes the song. The snare drum is, again, mixed very loudly to allow for the side stick and snare rolls to propel the track, while the bass line grounds the song. The use of delay is minimal, but the entire song sounds like it is floating in the clouds. The guitar skank is here as well and begins the rhythmic interplay on the album by being mixed low in the track.

The B-side of the album opens with B1 'Strictly Dub', which has the bass line and skank on the piano to begin the song. The drums then come in with another steppers pattern mixed with a focus on the snare and side stick hits. The song continues with the piano skank being mixed in and out with the delay that resonates through the album. The mix on the drums is again the most interesting thing in this track as the bass line stays strong and above the other elements in the track, except for the snare hits.

While this track starts the B-side, it also functions as a key marker in Bovell's style. The high hat is used again, like in A1, to propel the rhythm of the song while the bass drives it. The kick drum is mixed fairly low in the overall sound, and the delay is used on all of the elements. The timbre and feel of this track, along with 'Cut After Cut', demonstrate all of the ways that Bovell created his dubs at the beginning of his career.

B2 'Mint Ah Music' continues with similar stylistic elements of B1. Opening with a drum roll into the heavy bass timbre. This time, the bass line is matched with a delayed organ tone, and the piano skanks to open the song and is then delayed and mixed out. The keyboard that matches the bass line then starts diverging from the bass line a bit but quickly comes back to match it. The piano is the only instrument in this song that has a higher timbre, as the high at continues to ride the pattern throughout.

This song has another steppers pattern in the drums, with the side stick being delayed and manipulated throughout the track. The bass and keyboard line are the feature here, and the piano skank is delayed multiple times to float off into space. The keyboard line is morphed to sound bass heavy in tone but also like a strange-sounding alternative bass pattern.

Rhythmic interplay 7
A4 'River to Bank' shares similar elements to A2 in the rhythmic interplay and melody lines being used to build the song. The track begins with a drum intro but then has a melody line played on the piano that floats over the bass line. This time, the guitar plays a stick lead that matches the bass line as well. The sound of the piano is affected to have a lower timbre as well, and the drums play a one drop much like in 'Rebel Chase'.

There is a short organ bubble that sets the rhythmic interplay here as well with piano hits that come in and out of the track. All of which are put through the delay and equalised to a lower timbre. With the high hat and the guitar stick lead going throughout the song, the rhythmic interplay is demonstrated in the drums.

The A-side closes with A5 'Tell Yuh So', which shares a similar rhythmic interplay and writing style. This time, the melody is played on a keyboard that has a setting that reflects an outer space feel. The drums start the song again and play one drop but have more hits on the side of the snare here than the previously discussed songs. The keyboard is the focus of this track, playing the melody and then going into a solo over the heavy timbre of the bass line.

At 2:00 into the song, the keyboard plays a flush run that is delayed and repeats this again a few measures later. The late 1970's keyboard and digital technology can be heard on this track, and this is one of the starting points for the digital dub that would come in later years. The organ is completely washed in delay in the track, and the piano hits are processed through the delay as well. The guitar comes in to match the melody line in places and then reverts to a stick lead pattern between the bass notes. The end of the song has the keyboard flourishing between notes and then runs up and down.

Re-production 7
A3 'Ites of Dub' starts with a drum roll and goes right into a heavy bass line. The drums are affected through with reverb, and at 0:20, the re-production of the track becomes the focus as the drum hits are removed, and the delay is used to expand the hit as the bass

line plays. This is another steppers rhythm in the drums that allow for the bass line to play through and above the pattern of the song.

The re-production of this track is the focal point of it as the only two instruments in the track are the bass and drums. With the drums playing a busy pattern on the side stick, Bovell uses the delay to expand individual hits on the snare and the side of the snare. This expansion does not even sound like a drum at many times in the track as the hit is processed so much that it resonates differently in the timbre of the track. At 1:20, the snare hit is manipulated the most in this track as the rest of the track disappears. For purists of the dub genre, this is dub. Only bass and drums being used to construct a song that centres on the use of delay and re-production of the entire track to set a vibe and feel with the song.

B3 'Ska-Be-Doo-Za' is also demonstrative of Bovell's re-production of a dub. The drums roll into a beep bass line that is echoed by the keyboard, while the organ holds chords. Then the melody line rides over the steppers rhythm. The melody cuts out to allow the guitar and organ skank to continue through, and then the keyboard begins its solo over the track.

As the song continues, the piano and organ hits are put through the delay and warped till they dissolve. This takes a song that generally has a higher timbre and places it into a deeper register with effects carrying the re-production. At 2:40, the track begins to dissolve with the delay and the song fades out. This song begins the end of the album and suggests further constructive elements that will appear later in Bovell's catalogue.

B4 'Ah Weh' also shares similar constructive elements that frame Bovell's dubs. As the last track on the album, the bass timbre is set a bit higher here, but the use of the delay and reverb are prevalent. The drums start the song and play a stepper pattern with side stick hits coming through. The filters from the delay are also heard here in the high hat, and the piano hits are delayed and morphed out of recognition. The most interesting constructive element here is the play with the high hat. The bass is also mixed a bit lower in this song than others to give room for the other instruments to be processed and to become the focal point of this song.

The use of delay is centre at 2:55 in the track as the piano skank is destroyed by the delay, and the bass and drums continue. The song ends fading out with the delay continuing to be used. As stated above, the high hat being processed through a delay is extremely interesting in this song as the kick drum pattern stays straight. The high hat is warped out of time in places as the side stick of the snare is bouncing again, cutting through the track.

Completion 6

In the United Kingdom, dub becomes distilled from its original form and reframed into a new sound that is distinctly British. This new sound combined the pulse of the underground with the politics of the day and gave rise to a movement that still continues today. Starting with Keith Hudson, Dennis Bovell and others, the music shifted and became based on issues of class and race. Steel Pulse gave the sound a stage presence and gained a large following. Trojan records put the music into the popular charts and Island took it the rest of the way. The performative aspect of dub in the United Kingdom gave way to the sounds of contemporary society, and this created many different genres.

The importance of this distillation of sound cannot be overstated as many musicians and producers heard Jamaican sounds and styles and incorporated them into their own sound. Adrian Sherwood and Mad Professor continue to produce and put out records that challenge the meanings and sounds of dub. Dennis Bovell and Matumbi continue to perform around the world, and the culture of dub is being carried forward by many people in the sound system culture that has developed out of this starting point. Labels like Totally Dubwise and Bokeh Versions continue to supply the dance community with tracks. Oli Warwick (2018), in 'Dubbing is a must: The modern sound of leftified dub', states: 'Dedicated roots-minded soundsystem music has also prevailed. In the UK, the steppers scene rose out of the tireless work of Jah Shaka, Disciples, Jah Tubbys, Jah Warrior, Earthquake and many more' (n.pag.).

This new breed of DJs and producers has taken the music that was created by the original UK producers and manipulated it into a new sound that carries throughout the world. This can be viewed as another distillation of sound that is often argued as positive or negative within the culture of dub. The importance here is that the culture of dub continues to affect music around the world.

The spread of dub also led to UK Garage, grime and dubstep. All genres that begin with explorations of dub and roots music and blend with other forms of electronic music. Labels like Hyperdub, with Steve Goodman, aka Kode9 at the helm, further the work that Adrian Sherwood started by experimenting with soundscapes with African Head Charge and other groups. Again, these new genres are often argued and debated throughout the dub community, but dub's influence can be heard on every track.

What dub has become in the contemporary world is extremely interesting as it has progressed. What was once a music that was filled with space has drastically changed into different forms of dance music. This would not have happened without dub as a starting point and the original musicians, producers and engineers playing their role. Now, the concept of dub has returned to its roots again and has begun to gain more and more ground in England and, more importantly, Jamaica itself.

From the United Kingdom, dub gets transferred throughout the world. The culture can be seen in Indonesia, France, Spain, the Netherlands, Japan and anywhere else that dance culture is appreciated. The culture of dub and reggae in the United Kingdom spurred the formation of two-tone and the ska that was created led to an entire new form of popular music as well that blended the punk and reggae that was being heard. All through these changes, the dub was being listened to and championed as the sound and music that was listened to across genres. From punk to rock 'n' roll, dub became a part of the sonic landscape. This all began with the immigration of Jamaican artists, producers, DJs and musicians to England and spread throughout the world.

Chapter 7
Dub in New York City and the Hip Hop Generation

Another location for dub's distillation was New York City (NYC). Again, the immigration from Jamaica, Haiti and the West Indies led to people bringing their music and culture to the United States. What began as a way to connect with other immigrants, quickly developed into large street and house parties that would pave the way for rap and hip hop. Louis Chude-Sokei suggests that

> the intimacy of reggae and hip-hop is nothing more than a contemporary manifestation of tense and productive relationships established by a century of Caribbean immigration. New York, after all, has been a Caribbean city since very early on in this century and cultural forms like calypso owe much to New York and its recording studios early in the twentieth-century.
>
> (2018: 54)

With the arrival of Lloyd Barnes aka Bullwackie to the Bronx in 1967, reggae took a stronghold in America. There is a great deal written on the story and legacy of Wackie's, and the focus here will be on the sound of the label and how that sound and the sound system parties that were held brought dub to America and began many of the strategies that became hip hop. DJ Kool Herc, from Jamaica, is often stated as one of the originators of hip hop and was influenced by sound system and DJ culture growing up as well. These influences continue today with people like Carter Van Pelt,

Max Glazer, Dave Hahn, Dan Brenner, Bobby Konders, Jayson Nugent and Brett Tubin, to name a few.

The influence of Jamaican culture in NYC has turned the city into a focal point of reggae and Jamaican music around the world. VP Records still run their business out of New York, while others have moved out of the city. The influence of NYC reggae and dub cannot be overestimated, and it still holds a large part of the market. In the late 1970s, the NYC music scene was filled with disco and rock 'n' roll. Around 1972, Barnes opened Wackie's studio in a small space on 211th street and began recording vocalists over riddims that he had gained from his time in Jamaica working with Prince Buster and others. The sound of New York reggae begins here and the songs that were created have a distinct low-fi sound that became a signifier of New York style reggae and dub. Many people have been influenced by this style and continue to produce in ways that attempt to capture the style.

Wackie's mixing style is often said to relate to Lee 'Scratch' Perry's Black Ark sound, and it is this link that solidifies the connection between Jamaica and New York. A sparse studio, with limited effects processors, and a used mixing board, gave the studio its sound and feel. The key to this was Barnes' ear and feel for the music. A genuine love for the music that was not driven by money or glorified attempts at fame led to Wackie's being the influential force that it was. In 'The complete force: Wackies, a primer', Tim Wilson states:

> The peerless, enduring alchemy of Lloyd Bullwackie Barnes has been attributed to economical, analogue production and to the abundance of quality in the expat engineers and session players that surrounded him, but the decisive factors in why Barnes' sound continues to enthrall seems to be the basic elements of intuition and organic development.
>
> (n.d.: n.pag.)

This 'organic development' is not only the reason that people are enthralled by the sound, but it is what made New York reggae similar and different from Jamaica.

The similarities between the music that happened in both places stem from the concept of producing music with what was at hand. It did not matter about the latest technology or the most expensive recording gear in Jamaica or New York. The first engineers did what they could with what was around them and accessible and then built from there. Barnes was not different in this approach or thought process. Even the reuse of recorded tracks that he had from Jamaica with new vocalists and musicians was similar to the producers in Jamaica.

He was also extremely influenced by King Tubby and through witnessing sessions at Federal Records in Kingston with Duke Reid and Prince Buster. He discussed his links to King Tubby's style with Brandon Wilner in '40 years later reggae's heart still beats in the Bronx':

> 'He was the real king of dub; he set the pace', Barnes said. 'There was always a standard way to do a mix, but when he used effects and played with the vocal or drum track, there was real expression and courage. Seeing that gave me the picture of freedom'.
>
> (2020: n.pag.)

As others have stated, King Tubby is the root of dub and the key element here in the distillation of sound. Barnes states his appreciation of Tubby in almost every interview with a focus on the limited resources that were used to create such huge sounds.

Barnes' studio, originally, contained an Ampex 8-track recording console, a Moog synth, a DI box for the bass, and drums that were covered with cloth and aluminum foil, or so one source claims. A very simple setup for recording that relied on the engineer's ears and control of the equipment in order to obtain any type of sound. After a bit of time, the studio was moved to White Plains drive and the machinery grew as well. Barnes stated in the interview with Wilner in the *New York Times*,

> 'I'm just thankful I've gotten to make music how I want – a true feeling from within,' he said in an interview in the studio's break room, decorated with posters for international events and the label's original certificate of incorporation. 'When you do that for as long as I have, you're filled with gratitude'.
>
> (2020: n.pag.)

Another similarity between the New York sound and Jamaica lies in this 'true feeling from within' that is expressed by Barnes. This is what is important to dub and what transfers the music into and through the culture that it created. Many of the engineers that were involved in both places worked with the music because they felt they had to, or that it was their calling. This occurs in other forms of music as well, but the raw sounds of the engineer are heard in the music of dub. The sound print that is created and shared contains the feeling of the engineer.

Another strain that developed and continued to become hip hop was DJ culture championed by the DJs at the sound system parties. What would be championed by King Addies and Tony Matterhorn in the first wave of sound system parties began earlier when DJ Kool Herc came to NYC in 1967. Taking his inspiration from U-Roy and Big Youth during the ska and rocksteady years, Kool Herc brought the mixing and toasting style to the streets of NYC. For Clive Campbell, aka Kool Herc, the sound system parties in Jamaica influenced a revolution in sound.

The story of Campbell's first DJ set at his sister's birthday is legendary in hip hop circles. Playing music in the rec room of 1520, Sedgwick Ave would start his path and lead to his first professional job at the Twilight Zone in 1973. Trying to get into the club called Hevalo and getting rejected and then djing and competing with Zulu Nation and embarrassing Grandmaster Flash when he was first on the mic are all part of NYC's link to the Jamaican sound and culture. By using two of the same records and focusing on playing just the break section, Campbell created scratching and what would go on to become hip hop. He also coined the phrase b-boy, break boy, for the dancers who loved the break sections that he would play and can be credited with having the first hip hop MC when Coke La Rock grabbed the mic on his system.

The key to his sound was the volume and control over the different frequencies in the system. This was the link to Jamaican sound systems that he brought with him. His system was the loudest of all and continually beat out other systems for dominance of the club and dance floor. He could also easily manipulate the highs, mids and lows of the system to create different vibes within the club. This control brought the culture of Jamaica to NYC and created the bass heavy feel that would eventually lead to hip hop.

His first system was bought piece by piece and modeled off of a system he first saw at a show that was owned by The Amazing Bert. Campbell stated to Frank Broughton,

> I'm rolling with the big Mac [amp]. That cost like, say $1,600. A 2300 Mac, the biggest there is, the top of the line. The guy had top-of-the-line stuff. He had GLI, and the new company came out, he had the disco fours, and he had not one McIntosh 2300, he had two of them. And he had two [Altec] 'Voice of the Theatres' [speaker system].
>
> (cited in Broughton 2018: n.pag.)

He named his first system the Herculords and his second Not Responsible. With these systems, he brought the vibe of a Jamaican dance hall to the streets of New York and played music that the people wanted to hear.

One link between Herc and Bullwackie's was Imperial Jay Cee who would often visit Brad's Record Den record store and hung around the Herculords, sometimes referred to as Herculoids, sound system. He was one of the first DJs who developed scratching along with Clark Kent and Black Jack, who all came slightly after Coke la Rock and Kool Herc paved the way. Brad Osborne, who owned Clocktower records where Imperial Jay Cee and others worked, is another important link to Jamaica.

In 1971, Brad Osborne and Glen Adams, who was the organist for the Upsetters, opened up Clocktower records. They had a record store, Brad's Record Den, at 3756 White Plains road where Barnes and Jamaican immigrants flocked to. The start of reggae in NYC can be traced back to Osborne and Clocktower as well. It was here that the music continued and developed and then continued with the Chin family and VP Records.

Brad's Record Den was also a hangout of the people who would later become the first wave of hip hop. Roy Buckley (2015) stated in an interview: 'All them guys like Kool Herc, Afrika Bambaataa, and Grand Master Flash had been shopping at Brad's for years and Brad's was where they found a lot of the break beat records that they ended up making famous' (n.pag.). This is also where T-Ski Valley was 'discovered' and brought to the studio to record 'Catch the Beat', which is said to be the very first rap record. This would be released by Brad and Glen Adams on their Grand Groove Records label. The store was a place where people in New York could find calypso, reggae, soca, jazz and other forms of music that were not available elsewhere. This allowed the store to become a meeting place and a hub for the community, which led to the development of hip hop and rap.

The story of Osbourne and Clocktower takes a turn when he was gunned down in his store in 1986. Many people claim that Osbourne was releasing copies of material that the artists never received payment for. Clocktower was then bought by Alfred Abraham and the stories kept piling up. As important to the rise of reggae and hip hop in NYC and the world that Osbourne was, his legacy remains mixed within the dub community. His record store was one of the first to bring people together and, along with Wackie's studio, paved the way for dub and reggae in the United States and changed the world by inspiring hip hop. Another important element in the development of reggae and dub in the United States was, and still is, VP Records.

VP Records began in 1975 when Vincent 'Randy' Chin and his wife Patricia moved to New York from Jamaica and opened their record store, VP Records, in Brooklyn. The label began in 1979, and the store was later moved to Jamaica, Queens. They had started and owned Randy's record store and Studio 17 in Jamaica and were determined to spread Jamaican culture to the world. Vincent's son Clive Chin produced and co-wrote countless hit songs including Augustus Pablo's 'Java'. Carter VanPelt states in *Down in Jamaica: 40 Years of VP Records*:

> To establish a foothold in the New York area and build on the success of Vincent's brother Victor, who ran the successful Chin-Randy's shop on St. John's in Brooklyn, the Chin's used Vincent's sister Molly (Chin) Feliciano's Musicland shop at 328 Utica Ave for a handful of releases. Since there was already a Randy's Records in America, VP Records was the logical new name for the business as it got on its feet.
>
> (2019: 3)

The label continues to thrive and release music from reggae artists around the world. Seal Paul, Gyptian, Elephant Man, Beres Hammond, Morgan Heritage and many others are a part of the label.

Figure 7.1: 17 North Parade in 2018. Photo by author.

The story of Vincent Chin starting off selling and maintaining jukeboxes throughout Kingston is legendary. He started Randy's Record Mart in 1958 at 17 North Parade in Kingston and then opened Studio 17. Patricia Chin, O.D., known as Miss Pat, told Kayla Kush from *Rootfire*,

> The late fifties and the sixties were an exciting time because we had Dennis Brown, Peter Tosh, Bob Marley, Israel Vibration. Those were some singers that used the studio, and Lee Perry was always there using the studio, bringing new musicians and their artists and backup singers.
>
> (cited in Kush 2018: n.pag.)

VP Records in New York played a key role in the distillation of sound throughout the world and continues to do so today.

Many artists got their start through the Chin family, and many say that VP was the key to the development of Jamaican music in New York. This is true, especially from the 1980s to today as they continue to release new artists and new ideas. The history section from the VP website states:

> By staying true to their roots, VP Records has become a crucial link between reggae music and culture and an ever-growing market of reggae enthusiasts around the world. After over 30 years in the game, the Chin family looks forward to the future with confidence, knowing that they have built a business that is poised to take Caribbean culture to the highest heights.
>
> (Anon. 2019a: n.pag.)

When the family moved to New York, they had already become huge players in the music industry through the people who visited Randy's Record Mart and the artists who had recorded at Studio 17. Bob Marley and the Wailers, Peter Tosh, The Heptones, Dennis Brown, Burning Spear and many others recorded there and gave the VP label its reputation. The move to New York was to expand the market for Jamaican music and it did.

> During the first five years in New York, VP developed a variety of sublabels including Love, Roots, Roots From The Yard, Jah Guidance, Lightning, and Reggae Sound. VP helped establish the sound of the 'early dancehall' period of the 1980s, featuring artists such as Yellowman, Michigan & Smiley, Johnny Osbourne, Michael Prophet, and Barrington Levy. Hits such as 'Zunguzunguguzeng', 'Diseases', 'Ice Cream Love', 'Gun Man', and 'Prison Oval Rock' highlighted the era.
>
> (Anon. 2019b: n.pag.)

Today, VP carries the torch of reggae throughout the world and is considered by many to be the largest and best label for reggae and Jamaican music. The Chin family continues to play a large role in the operations of the label even as Vincent has passed on and Miss Pat has retired and has assumed matriarchal status. VP continues to distill the Jamaican sound throughout the world with many different satellite businesses and labels. Their recent purchase of the Greensleeves label assures that classic recordings will also be saved and put back out into the market for future listeners to enjoy.

Wackie's, Brad's Record Den and VP Records all start the expansion of reggae not only to New York but also around the world. VP still produces reggae, in all genres, and has survived the many changes of the industry while the others have shifted or faded away in time. The influence of Jamaican music in New York began the distillation of sound to the rest of the world and, along with the UK, contributed to the continued importance of Jamaican music.

Social 8

Like many urban areas, NYC in the 1970s had its share of street crime and violence. Gangs such as the Black Spades, Savage Skulls, the Dirty Ones, Roman Kings, Ghetto Brothers, the Savage Nomads, the Tomahawks and many more protected their area and were divided by race and ethnicity. These gangs generally consisted of kids and young adults who were trying to protect their neighborhood and to establish a name for themselves. In a *Vice* article titled, 'How the gangs of 1970s New York came together to end their wars', John Surico (2015) writes:

> This is what the Bronx looked like in the early 1970s: a battleground filled with gangs of all shapes and sizes in a vaguely moderated state of anarchy, turf wars fueled by the economic failure of shoddy urban planning in a city verging on bankruptcy.
> (n.pag.)

The division between social classes was pronounced in the city during this time and led to the development of gangs fighting to survive.

Basing their organisation on the Hell's Angels, the gangs followed strict organisation and rules. They also used the Native American, Apache, markings for territory. The importance of these groups lies in the community-building aspect of organisation. Even though many were involved in illegal activities and clashed with one another often, they gave people a sense of belonging and a feel of community that was desperately needed at the time. Gary Warnett (2016), in 'How the Block Party invented hip hop', stated: 'In late 1971, however, a gang truce – the Hoe Avenue Peace Meeting – liberated what was once a patchwork of guarded territories, breaking down the barriers between blocks' (n.pag.).

This truce is highlighted in documentaries and became a turning point in the city of New York's development and continuation.

The area where Wackie's was located and having borders of White Plains road to the east and the Bronx River to the West is called Soundview. This is the area where reggae and hip hop developed. The Black Spades were the gang that formed here beginning in 1968 in the Bronxdale Houses. Originally named the Savage Seven, this gang was influenced by the teachings of the Nation of Islam, the Black Panthers and Weather Underground. Afrika Bambaataa was said to be a warlord in a division of the gang and Kool Herc states that the Black Spades, Savage Skulls, Glory Stompers, Blue Diamonds and Black Cats played a part in creating hip hop as they were all going to the clubs.

Osbourne and others were all familiar with, and some associated with, these gangs. This is not the area to state who was a part of what, but more to demonstrate the links and importance of these gangs to the development of reggae and dub music in NYC. One of the first DJs in the Bronx was DJ Mario, who spun mostly funk and disco. He was an early member of the Black Spades and could also be credited with starting hip hop. According to Seba Kwesi Damani Agyekum, in 'A history of hip hop in perspective',

> Mario was able to serve in this capacity because he had the 'hook-up' and 'controlled' access to the schools, especially JHS 123, which was the main place where they threw parties in the Bronxdale projects. Anybody that played in neighborhood schools had to come through Mario.
>
> (2018: 3)

To be able to throw a street party, you had to have connections to the Black Spades or other gangs to be protected from theft and other incidences. It was these street parties that gave rise to hip hop.

There are many people that discuss the link between Jamaican sound system culture and hip hop, and these links are there, but they are more in cultural influence and not as direct as some have claimed. Veal states in his work:

> Sonically and aesthetically, musicians like DJ Kool Herc essentially transplanted the Jamaican sound system model to New York

City, along with the concept of mobile entertainment, which, for a brief moment in the late 1970s, was able to rearticulate urban space in a new, class-inflected way in the form of the neighborhood block party.

(2007: 247)

The majority of records played at these first parties were funk and then disco, not reggae. The importance of this is that version and dub played a bigger role in giving DJs like Kool Herc and others inspiration to be able to play with the music. Without the culture of dub, and its manipulation of music, break beat and other forms of mixing may not have occurred. Agyekum (2018) states: 'It was not just the songs he played but how he played them that made his set unique. It was a new way of "playing" music, one centered on highlighting a particular part of an existing song' (6). The Jamaican influence comes through in the control of the music.

This control created break beat and b-boy culture and is directly related to the manipulation that dub engineers did to the tracks. Herein lies the connection and relationship between the two types of music and the new sound that developed out of it. Herc using funk records to entice people to dance and Osbourne and Wackie's creating and distributing reggae and dub music influenced hip hop and the culture of rap.

There were many other influences in the development of hip hop, and it is not to say that the Jamaican influence is the only one. It did, however, lend inspiration and a creative way to use the music to move the crowd. Would hip hop exist without Jamaica? Probably, but the links and timing of the shift in culture were a large part of why records were used in a different way. DJ Kool Herc changed the way that people used records to entertain the crowd and also shifted the ways in which people heard music. Much like the original engineers, the sound system owners and DJs did in Jamaica.

The first release by the BullWackie's All Stars came out on Aries records in 1975 and was titled *Free for All*. It was re-released on Basic Channel in Germany in 2007. The Bullwackie All Stars consisted of many musicians that included Jerry Harris, Ras Menelik, Jerry Johnson, Clive 'Azul' Hunt and Douglas Levy. The main engineers were Douglas Levy and Junior Delahaye. Along with Lloyd Barnes producing, this album showcased the dub and sounds that were possible at Wackie's. The tracklist for this album is A1 'Free for All', A2 'Space Age', A3 'Roots', A4 'Drum Call', A5 'Tribal Dub', B1 'All for Free', B2 'Dis-Ya-a-Dub', B3 'Boma-ya-Dub', B4 'Meditation Dub' and B5 'Blackbyrd'.

Timbre 8

The timbre in the entire album is dark and somewhat ominous. This was the sound of NYC being heard through the reggae that was being manipulated. The key difference between Wackie's sound and others was the raw edge that was obtained through his studio. The sounds distort in many places, and the mix is not perfect, but the feel of the city comes through. When you listen to this album, you get a sense and feel of 1970s and 1980s NYC.

The first track A1 'Free for All' opens the album with a bass line that was mixed to the point of distortion throughout the track. The drums roll the song in, and the melody line is carried by the guitar throughout the track. There is a minimal amount of fader moves in this track, as all of the different tracks seem to be pushed to their max. This was the Wackie's style, a floating guitar over an extremely loud bass line. This song begins the album with a feel of being recorded live in one take with all of the musicians playing at the same time, and the engineer recording as the song is played. This was a different way of composing and creating dub that allows for the musicianship to carry the track.

The drums are also interesting in this track as they are mixed very low, compared to other dub mixes. The high hat is the loudest in the mix, but the distortion in the bass line covers the kick drum in most parts. The snare hits and side stick are heard when they are played, and the kick drum is prominent in some parts to match the bass line. The sound of this track resonates with a limited studio and one that is recording in a specific style.

As stated before, the musicianship was the key to the success of the dub. Without players who could create reggae that grooved and was easy to manipulate, there would be nothing to dub. The first track of this album demonstrates the quality of the musicians in Wackie's studio, but also the distinct attempt to produce a raw and unaffected tone to the music.

A2 'Space Age' opens with a reverbed line and then the song starts but pulls up quickly to begin again. You can hear the feedback of the studio tape machine in the beginning of the track.

You can also hear the guitarist pick up the guitar right before the line starts. The main melody is carried through the song and lays over the entire track. The interesting thing again is that the music is extremely pushed in the recording. You can hear the piano line hitting upbeats at points, but the mix is stable and does not fluctuate like other dub records. The liveness of this track is the timbre, and the dirtiness of the song allows the listener to seemingly be in the studio.

At around 1:02, the track even splits and seems to have been poorly spliced together in an edit. The song drops off in the middle of the melody line and restarts with it again, but the hiccup that this creates is extremely interesting in that this would not have been released at another studio this way. The track ends abruptly as well suggesting an edit that was done to the rhythm tracks. This is all part of the timbre of Wackie's and allows for us to hear the history of this studio on tape.

A3 'Roots' begins with a horn hit and a horn line with a trumpet and a saxophone playing over the rhythm. Then the horns drop out and the bass and drums ride with the horns coming in with various hits and accents. The drums are heard here, and the timbre of this track is brighter, but still has the grittiness of the Wackie's sound. The side stick of the snare is affected with a reverb unit in this track as well, which is different from the other songs on the album, and the song is shortcoming in at only 2:22 in length.

The timbre of this track becomes interesting in demonstrating what horns sounded like in Wackie's studio. This sound is one that demonstrates the limited number of mics and editing that was used in constructing the horn lines. This was a live band playing at the same time or two horns playing together into one or two microphones. The way that the snare is mixed through the reverb unit keeps the song rooted in a darker tone even though the horns are bright and forward in the mix.

Rhythmic interplay 8

A4 'Drum Call' begins with a pulse on the drums linking to Nyabinghi, and this carries through the track as the song continues. There are also fader moves here, or the band starts and stops during the recording, to give the drums space in the song. The congas and bongos on this track are the standouts as the guitar is used for the rhythmic interplay with the chuck-a form. The darker tone of the bass drum propels the song as well. The piano is heard in the upbeats, and the organ bubbles when the full track comes in. At 1:45, the full song comes in and the auxiliary percussion also begins and is mixed on top of the song. Then the main instruments are cut to allow the drums to finish the track on their own.

While this style of drumming was common in reggae music at this point, the way that this mix centres on the drums and has them improvising is important. The main melody instruments are mixed in and out of the track around the drums, and this centres the percussion instruments as the focal point in the rhythmic interplay of the song.

The first side of the record ends with A5 'Tribal Dub', which contains the first vocals to appear on the record. A dub of the song 'Tribal War' by John Holt, this version lets the lyrics begin the dub and then cuts them to have the bass line and drums carry the song. An example of the mixing style of Wackie's studio is demonstrated here, and the rhythmic interplay throughout the track changes to be held by a saxophone, guitar and organ. The original recording does not have a saxophone on the track. The bass line is also pushed again to the point of distortion and Holt's vocal appears in different places in the mix of the song.

This track suggests the re-use of a song in a different way to create a new song. The riddim side of dub is demonstrated here as the musicians play with and over an existing song to create a new track, while the engineer mixes the tracks to form the dub version. The saxophone is the key to this track as it is different from the original and is heard as a new addition. Then focusing on the way that the vocals come in and out of this version is also interesting. The bass line and kick drum distorting around 1:54 also allow the listener to hear Wackie's sound and timbre.

Re-production 8

The B-side of the record opens with 'All for Free', B1, a dub version of the opening track 'Free for All'. In this track, you hear the way that the engineer is manipulating the original song's instrument tracks. The bass line is not as distorted, and the guitar melody is prominent. There is not a great deal of modification to the original song, but this version is better mixed and sounds much clearer to the listener. The distortion on the bass and the grittiness is still within this track, but the guitar dominates this track instead of the bass line. The question becomes, was this a different mix and they decided to use both or was this an intended version of the song. Only Bullwackie and the people who created this song know this.

B2 'Dis-Ya-a-Dub' is a dub version of a Wackie's single that was originally released as 'A-Dis-Ya-A-Dub' on the Aries imprint by Munchi and the Corner Crew in 1974. Here it gets a full dub treatment and is constructed to reuse the original song. The track on *Free for All* starts with the same piano line and then cuts everything except the bass and drums. The vocals are removed here, and the bass carries the track. In the original, the vocals play in and out over the bass line with 'A rub, a dub, A dis-ya-a dub'. The re-production of this dub is also interesting in the reuse of the same version that appears on the B-side of the single. The original version is much brighter in tone, while this version is darker and pushes the bass to the front more, but the variations are similar in other constructive elements.

The bass line leading the melody of the track is essential in dub versions, and this track is no different from other simple dub versions. What is different is that this track demonstrates the studio's reuse of a popular single from their catalog on a full-length release. The choice to create another version and to not include the original vocal version is very interesting in that it may suggest that the focus on the musicians was key or that the tracks were owned by the studio and vocals were not.

B3 'Boma-Ye-Dub' references the fight between George Foreman and Muhammad Ali in 1974 in which Ali won by knockout and the crowd shouted 'Ali, bomaye!', which translates to 'Ali, Kill Him' from Bantu. The track starts off with a horn line and carries the lightest tone on the record. The bass is not pushed here as in the other tracks, and the grittiness is hear, but the re-production is the most interesting thing on this track. If you listen closely, you can hear a vocal cue that is either bleed from the room mics or mixed almost completely out.

This vocal suggests the feel of the fight and possibly what being in the boxing match would have felt like with the crowd yelling for you. Barely hearing the chant but feeling it as the fight progresses. The horns accenting the melody line of the bass and the piano playing the same line as the bass propels the song. The drum part is also propulsive in that the high hat is mixed at the top, and the rest of the kit is barely heard in this track.

B4 'Meditation Dub' is one of the most effective dubs, in terms of re-production, on this album. The track begins with a vocal call out along with the guitar melody line and then dissolves into a heavy bass and drum part that continues through the song. The piano is faintly heard to give the song some rhythmic interplay as well. The piano also comes in to accent the bass line with fader moves that are put through an effects processor. The bass is pushed to the point of distortion again, and the lo-fi nature and grittiness come through on the entire track.

This track resonates as one of the key dubs in the Wackie's catalog as all of the sounds of the studio and fader moves are heard within it. The darkness of the sound is here, and the rhythmic interplay also comes through in ways with the piano and guitar coming in to accent the beat. The drums are also mixed in the Wackie's style with the high hat being loud and the kick being distorted. This track is a key song in demonstrating the Wackie's sound.

B5 'Blackbyrd' closes the album and shares the traits discussed above with 'Meditation Dub'. It begins with a drum roll and the bass being pushed to the extreme. The vocal line comes in and is mixed loud enough to hear but competes with the bass line. This is then dropped out to allow just the bass and drums to continue. The high hat is the loudest part of the drum set in the mix as the vocals are faded in and out throughout the track. The fader moves on the guitar are also interesting as they propel the melody in parts and are then quickly cut out. What is consistent here is the harsh, driving bass line pushed to the extreme limit.

Completion 7

Free for All demonstrates what happens in a limited studio with great musicians coming together to create and record. There are many more singles and albums that were released from Wackie's, but this one contains all of the elements of the sound of NYC reggae in the 1970s before the digital revolution. The dark tones and grittiness of each track were the attempt at sounding like the Jamaican releases that were influential to Barnes and the recording style was as well. These songs, unfortunately mostly not hits, influenced countless numbers of listeners who would go on to become legends in Hip Hop, reggae and dub. With Glen Adams and Linval Thompson, Barnes became one of the first people to open up a reggae label in the United States. Capo, Thompson Sound and Wackie's began the distillation of reggae and dub in America, and *Free for All* still resonates as a distinct moment in classic reggae.

The influence of Wackie's can be seen today throughout NYC and the world. In New York, particularly the record store, Jammyland carried on the tradition and worked closely releasing material from the Wackie's label. Many people continue to create dub and spin reggae music throughout the city on any night of the week. People like Dave Hahn, with Dub is a Weapon, Dan Brenner, under the name 100 decibels and Soon Come, Subatomic Soundsystem, Jayson Nugent, with Crazy Baldhead, Carter Van Pelt with VP Records, Bobby Konders, Max Glazer, King Addies, Victor Rice, Victor Axelrod aka Tiklah and many others continue to spread the message of dub and reggae music in New York and around the world.

Dave Hahn formed the band Dub is a Weapon in 2001 as a group that performed live dub. Much like Matumbi and others, the music was dubbed by Hahn on stage as it was played. Hahn had played with many ska groups in NYC like Skinnerbox, Stubborn All Stars and the Slackers, played afrobeat with Antibalas, and was the engineer for the Easy Star All Stars *Dub Side of the Moon* tour. Through all of this, he wanted to put together a live dub act and the group was formed.

Dub is a Weapon was also the backing band for Lee 'Scratch' Perry in 2005–07. This link was the pinnacle for Hahn, who began listening to dub because of the jazz like improvisation of the engineer at the mixing board. He began getting his dub records at Jammyland and searching for everything on the Blood and Fire record label after finding the Greensleeves Scientist collections and the pivotal *Scientist Wins the World Cup* record. Hahn is an example of the new group of musicians and engineers in New York that propelled the music into the contemporary world. His consistent take on the music remains rooted in the sound of the older dub artists and engineers. By keeping similar tones and sounds, Dub is a Weapon continues to dive into the dub of the past with a modern feel.

After moving to a space in Greenpoint, Brooklyn that had room for a studio, Hahn had time and access to experiment with dub mixing. Hahn states: 'I had friends come over and record tracks, and when I say friends, I'm talking about Victor Rice, Eddie

Ocampo, Sheldon Gregg [...] and I kind of mixed and matched musicians to get tracks that I could dub out' (2020). These were all phenomenal musicians from the NYC ska scene, most of whom are still playing and releasing music today. With the tracks they created, and other horn players from Antibalas, Hahn began dubbing and experimenting in the studio to get sounds that mimicked King Tubby.

'If there was somebody in New York that I think is a genius dub producer, that I got excited about working with and knowing, it was Victor Axelrod, Tiklah' (Hahn 2020). Axelrod released *Polydemic* in 1998 and *Hi-Fidelity Dub Sessions: Roots Combination* in 2001 before working with Mark Ronsen on Amy Winehouse's *Back to Black* record and many other famous recordings. He was a key player in Antibalas and released *Ticklah Vs. Axelrod* on Easy Star Records label in 2007.

Dub is a Weapon toured with Lee 'Scratch' Perry and Hahn discussed how Perry was received throughout the country as a showman. A show at the House of Blues in L.A. brought out many famous people and demonstrated how large dub could be throughout the country. Again, this connection is a key development in the distillation of sound that occurred with dub. Hahn states: 'Dub is a musical genre that offers a bunch of possibilities' (2020), as he takes this music into a contemporary format with an older feel.

Another contemporary member of the dub and sound system scene in New York is Dan Brenner, aka Soon Come and 100 dbs. Under these monikers, Dan has developed a reputation as a sonic engineer who manipulates electronics to create songs. He is an example of the engineer creating dub within the scene and continues to add new sounds and energy to the culture of dub music. Starting as a guitarist and playing music in the ska and rocksteady scene in NYC, Dan soon found he preferred engineering the music.

Along with this drive to engineer the music, Brenner discussed Bobby Konders as one of the most important elements of the contemporary NYC scene. Konders became famous in the underground dance music scene of the 1980s before forming his Massive B Soundsystem with his partner Jabba in the 1990s. He gained international fame as the DJ in the video game *Grand Theft Auto IV*. Konders is still DJing and keeping reggae alive in New York and around the world. Along with Max Glazer, Carter VanPelt and others, the reggae scene continues to thrive. 'But if you talk about

New York, in and along that same vein of like early 90s crossover vibe. I kind of consider that in the family of dub' (Brenner 2020). Brenner states that reggae and mashup culture in New York was a part of keeping dub alive and gaining strength in the city.

Brenner holds Konders up as an influence when listening to the dub and versions that he produced for the B-sides of records and for mixtapes. Brenner continues to spin at reggae on the boardwalk and other events in the city as well. His focus for Soon Come lies in working with foundation riddims and reworking them with electronics and samplers. 'If I can make some simple, but good, 80s sounding digital rhythms, then I could bring a small box to the dance and have DJs jump on the production and they are ready for it' (Brenner 2020).

Here is where dub and reggae still meet, in the dance hall. Wackie's and VP Records began a culture that continues today with reggae and dance hall, while dub, both version and full dub, continues with groups like Dub is a Weapon, Soon Come and others. As Brenner states: 'The key to dub is that it is a process' (2020). It is this process that links the newer people with the old as they focus on the engineering aspect of the music and continue to propel dub into the contemporary world. Without Wackie's to begin this journey, and Jammyland to act as the discovery point, these individuals would not have had the same experience with dub music.

The contemporary movement of dub and reggae in NYC was framed around the record store Jammyland. Located at 60 East 3rd street in Manhattan from 1993 to 2008, this store became the central gathering point for reggae and dub in the city. Ira Heaps, Malcom Allen and Ras Kush were the founders of the store and the recording studio that was in the basement hosted The Slackers, Victor Rice and many others. Jayson Nugent, Crazy Baldhead and guitarist for the Slackers worked at Jammyland for years as well. This was where people like Hahn and Brenner found dub records and expanded their collections.

This was also a hang out where people from all walks of life would visit. Much like a contemporary version of Wackie's record store, Jammyland worked closely to carry all of Wackie's releases. In Brandon Wilner's article, '40 years later reggae's heart still beats in the Bronx', he writes:

> Ira Heaps of the now-defunct East Village record store Jammyland met Barnes when his shop became an outlet for some

Figure 7.2: Jammyland street in New York City. Photo: Courtesy of Ira Heaps.

[of] Wackie's pressings done in 1998. For Heaps, the label captured a distinct New York spirit. 'The dark, sparse sound was what I loved,' he wrote in an email. 'New York was a great place in the '70s and '80s. It was dangerous, but full of soul. That whole vibe definitely found its way into the music'.

(2020: n.pag.)

Jammyland began after Ira Heaps had worked in a studio called Noise New York. As a bass player and sound engineer for many clubs and bands, Heaps took to dub after a realisation that the engineer was the focus of the music.

I would do a lot of live sound, here in the Lower East Side, in all these little clubs and stuff like that. Nobody really took the sound guy seriously; you know what I'm saying ... Here's a whole genre of music that worships the sound guy. The engineer is the star.

(Heaps 2020)

In a discussion with Heaps, Jammyland was a place where so many people gathered and used to meet up with others. The connections that were made at the store benefited many people.

Jammyland began through Heaps' travels to Jamaica, specifically Westmoreland and other areas by Negril in the 1980s. He told the story of visiting and getting involved in the area and stated:

My slogan at the time was 'What's the Jammy?' and I would just, like, walk up to people and be like 'Hey, What's the Jammy?' So, the Jamaicans named me Jammyman. And then the joke became Jammyman from Jammyland, Hence, the birth of the name. Jammyland.

(Heaps 2020)

After the opening of the store, Heaps eventually met Barnes and the connection began.

Barnes and Heaps met after Jammyland started selling represses of Wackie's records.

We hit it off pretty well and we did a lot of work together. Studio work, you know, he worked in my studio, and he wanted me to be the U.S. representative. Then the Germans got involved and I kind of let them have it.

(Heaps 2020)

This connection demonstrates the importance of Jammyland to the continuation of dub and reggae in New York. Heaps was also involved with Ari Up, which is an entire book as well, but his work with her was pivotal in the New York reggae scene.

The group that was formed, through a connection made by Vic Ruggerio, was Ari Up and the True Warriors and Heaps became the bandleader. '[Ari] wanted to get something going on, and I was interested', says Heaps (2020). 'Jamaican music was a huge part in Ari's life, and one of the things we connected on greatly was the fact that we both really knew Jamaica, the culture, the

Figure 7.3: Jammyland sign. Photo: Courtesy of Ira Heaps.

language' (Heaps 2020). The band would go on to tour Europe and eventually disband around 2008. The importance here is that Heaps was a part of continuing the reggae scene in multiple ways, along with owning a space where the scene developed and arguably began.

Heaps tells the story about how the UK steppers and Digidub scene got to New York through Jammyland as well. The importance here is that Jammyland was not only fixated on rereleases and the past. While that was a large part of the store and market, Heaps was influential in exposing New York and America to the Digidub scene from the UK. 'We had a great, great, effect on the community and it became international ... We started a whole movement of UK Digidub, you know, In New York. It was pretty amazing' (Heaps 2020). Jammyland became the place to go for reggae in New York, and many connections were made at the store.

Jammyland was a continuation of what Wackie's began and led to many people finding and developing a love for reggae and dub music. It also became a place for musicians to gather with a recording studio in the basement of the record store around 2003. Jayson Nugent, who worked there and helped build the studio, stated that the area was still a bit shady in the early 1990s, but right across the street was the Hell's Angels clubhouse. The store was opened during a time where CDs were the format of choice and selling records was an act of conserving the vinyl format. Discussing what made Jammyland special Nugent stated:

> Just the collection of people working there, you know. It was like weirdos like me just getting into reggae and dub, and then there was like Ras Kush, and then other people just coming through. People like Milton Henry, Glen Browne, and they would do in store performances or meet and greets. Luciano, Lynval Thompson, Leroy Smart, they would just pass through.
>
> (2020)

This was right before the internet took over and Jammyland was a place to find out about parties or the next event that was going to be held in the reggae and dub underground. Nugent stated: 'In New York, it was suddenly like hip to be into dub in the late 90s. It became, like, a cool thing to be a part of' (2020). During this time, there were regular DJ nights at places like Joe's Pub and the Raven where Ras Kush, Nugent and others would spin reggae and dub. With the studio being built in the basement, and guidance from Jeff Baker, aka King Django, Nugent could record anyone who was in town for tracks to produce and dub. 'I was like one of the few people who had keys. It was Django, Me, Vic Ruggerio, and Vic Rice. So, I would just go over their whenever I was bored and just throw on some tape' (Nugent 2020). This was the continuation of dub and reggae music that would eventually lead to Crazy Baldhead. Jammyland was the key in these developments.

The link between Wackie's and Jammyland allowed for the New York reggae and dub scene to continue and flourish. Along with Ernie B's and Channel One outside of Manhattan, Jammyland carried the records and the vibe that pushed the scene into the contemporary world. Ira Heaps and John III were critical pieces to the distillation of sound through their record sales and represses of Wackie's and other key Jamaican records. The store became a fixture and destination for anyone visiting NYC and still holds a nostalgic place for many people in the scene.

Wackie's was also paramount in the distillation of the sound to Japan as Wackie's Far East Chapter was started in 1999 with Ras Takashi. The tour that began this label would lead to some of the largest gatherings of people interested in reggae and dub that Japan had ever seen. The inspiration then led to others forming and developing the sound further into what has become a huge force in dub and reggae music.

Reggae in New York was built through the communities that were involved in bringing the Jamaican style and feel to the city. These communities embraced and revolved around the culture of Jamaica and the music that was created. This community feel continues today in New York and around the world. From the beginnings of the distillation through the development of hip hop to dance hall and contemporary roots reggae, New York has played a role in every way. VP Records is still dominating the major label charts with artists like Jah 9 and Gyptian and continues to garner Grammy Nominations. This is all due to the foundations in Jamaica and how the music shaped the culture in New York.

Chapter 8
Japan and the Rising Sound of Dub

Figure 8.1: Stack of speakers in Tony Meyer's yard. Photo: Courtesy of Cassandra Abbey (2019).

Distillation of Sound

In Japan, the distillation of dub culture began in the 1970s and continues today making Japan one of the largest places for dub music and sound system culture in the world. The way in which the sound and culture have been assimilated into the Japanese community is an amazing thing to discuss. Through well-known record labels like Riddim Chango, Rough Signal and Overheat, sound systems like Rankin Taxi, to contemporary sounds like Deadly Dragon Sound and Mighty Crown, Japan has become the leader in sound system culture. In terms of dub music, this is a bit different as the style and sound of reggae in Japan shift from the beginning to today. The way that reggae came to Japan is similar to other parts of the world with Bob Marley leading the way. The key link in the distillation of dub and reggae was the promotion company Tachyon in Japan, which was affiliated with Bullwackies in NYC. Mighty Massa formed Mighty Massa Soundsystem in 1994 and exploded the culture into what it is today. Nahki founded the first 'Japansplash' in 1981 and recorded 'Original Ninja' in 1989 with Prince Jammy in Jamaica. The band Mute Beat, along with Fishmans, were the first reggae bands in Japan and the first to create dub records. Dry and Heavy and many others also continue to perform dub in Japan.

Reggae in Japan began when Bob Marley came to the country to perform and tour in 1979. This moment led to many people feeling a connection to the music and style of Jamaica. In Rob Schenck's (2019) article 'Land of the rising dread: Five decades of sound system culture in Japan', he writes:

> 'Many of the older reggae fans I know in Japan speak of how Marley's "rebel spirit" captivated them during his first tour. His dreadlocks, his revolutionary thinking seemed in such opposition to the prevailing conformist culture of Japan at the time,' says Jeremy Freeman, veteran DJ and owner of Deadly Dragon Sound System.
>
> (Schenck 2019: n.pag.)

This feeling of connection is often mentioned when discussing reggae in other parts of the world. The style and beat are part of this connection, but the link to the people is the key. It is a rebel feeling, but also something that can somewhat safely be consumed through music.

There is an interesting distinction that occurs when Jamaican music meets Japanese aesthetic and feel. The two forms of culture are seemingly disparate, yet the music and vibe are shared. The ways in which the music is distilled in Japan are also different as the focus, from the beginning, was to insert Japanese sounds and feel into a Jamaican music. When this occurred in England, it was met with disdain and criticism, whereas in Japan, it was celebrated. This occurs in other forms of popular culture as well, but reggae is an interesting point of discussion. Here, the focus is on the ways in which the music has shaped and inserted itself to become part of the Japanese culture. Simon Frith (1987) discusses this insertion in 'Towards an aesthetic of popular music', and states: 'The question we should be asking is not what does popular music *reveal* about "the people" but how does it *construct* them' (137, emphasis added). The dub of Japan is a distinct type that plays with Japanese roots music and cultural sounds added to the backbeat and feel of Jamaican music. This is not the case with every band but was attempted by most.

This re-production did not happen only in Japan. It is this link that frames all of the distillation of sound throughout the world. Frith's discussion on the ways in which music builds 'the people' centres this distillation in Japan. The ways in which the Japanese people took the sound of Jamaica into their world is paramount here. The use of Patois and ways of presenting self in Japan through Jamaican images and ideals are also extremely interesting. The culture heard and saw the music and began asserting a Japanese ideal into it that created a different distillation than what had happened in England and America.

Social 10

The argument continues with concepts of assimilation and cultural appropriation, but that is not for this discussion. The ways that the music became part of Japanese culture through the incorporation of sounds and creative ways of combining the music is the point here. David Katz (2014a) states:

> Japan is a beguiling place in many ways, and although it may seem contradictory that reggae would be so highly embraced in a nation with so few black people, Japanese devotees obviously take

reggae very seriously – perhaps more seriously than any other non-Jamaican audience on earth.

(n.pag.)

This statement is the key to the discussion on reggae in Japan. The focus on every detail of Jamaican culture and life in reggae circles in Japan drives the distillation of sound. It is more than just the music for these followers. It is about becoming a part of the sound.

The magazine *Strive* was instrumental in developing and growing the reggae scene as they translated the lyrics into Japanese for the audience. The DJ scene that developed in reggae and dance hall was also key to the interpretation and understanding of the sound system culture. It is important to note that dub is surpassed in Japan by this sound system and dance-hall culture, but there are still many groups and engineers performing and adding dub elements to the stage and recordings.

Strive is owned by Mighty Crown and is a free paper magazine distributed at shows and throughout the scene. The importance of the translated lyrics cannot be overstated. It was in the lyrics that many Japanese people began to understand and relate to the music. The complete distillation of the sound of Jamaica occurred when the Japanese MCs began to incorporate Patois with Japanese during sound system parties. By translating the lyrics of reggae songs for the people, *Strive* and others influenced generations of enthusiasts.

Language is an extremely important part of the distillation of reggae around the world. In Japan, language is a key to opening the viewpoints of the singers and MCs. It is also important to understand that the mimicking of style and language is almost always in appreciation, not harm. This is very different in other countries where the appropriation of language and style sometimes reflects negatively. In Japanese reggae and dub circles, it is essential to understand and utilise the language that the original music is recorded in. This also occurs with English language songs and other forms of music. The Japanese person who understands and knows the original language of the song is seen as more knowledgeable and more closely linked to the source.

This is where the argument between assimilation and appropriation takes place. In this discussion, I will refer to Sterling's work on the use of Jamaican Patois and Rastafarian religious symbols in Japanese club scenes. Here, the focus is on how the sound of dub and reggae gets mixed with Japanese aesthetic and feel to form a Japanese dub. The combination of styles and what this affects is the point. How did the distillation of sound lead to the creation and furthering of Jamaican culture in Japan? One of the easiest ways to see this is in dance-hall music and forms in Japan.

The dance hall of Japan is famous for winning international and Jamaican sound clashes with Mighty Crown leading the way and winning dance-hall queen competitions with Junko carrying the torch throughout the world. Are these mere copies of the Jamaican scene and dance? Are they distilling the sound and culture too much? When discussing these issues with Jamaicans, the conversation quickly revolves back to the point that Jamaica needs to step up their game to compete and win and to 'take back' what has been stolen from them. Again, this is a conversation for a different book, but it centres on the fact that the music has been consumed thoroughly in Japan.

In the book *Babylon East: Performing Dancehall, Roots Reggae, and Rastafari in Japan*, Marvin Sterling (2010) discusses the beginnings of reggae in Japan and how it caught on. He states:

> Tokyo's Club 69, established early in the first period (mid-1970s–early-1980s), is credited with being the first such establishment; this regularly packed club, which played only roots reggae, was run by Jah K. S. K., one of several Japanese who were part of the hippie scene before becoming attracted to reggae and Rasta culture.
>
> (Sterling 2010: 10)

The Bob Marley concert tour in 1979 is also often cited as the beginning of reggae in Japan. Many people saw this tour, and the spark was lit for the formation of bands and clubs.

Sterling also addresses the issue of cultural appropriation in his work and very nicely puts it by stating:

> Is there a realistic scenario in which Japanese today can avoid engaging in structural racism in their adoptions of Jamaican culture? For me, the short answer is no. This is as true for the Japanese as it is for anyone else who engages the cultural

production of politically marginalized racial others with a structurally facilitated indifference to the opinions of these racial others (as seen in anything from tourism to some approaches to anthropology, past and present).

(2010: 27)

The issue for this discussion is not if this appropriation is wrong or racially motivated, but in how the music transferred and became a mix of Jamaican and Japanese sounds. He continues stating: 'The uncomfortable gap between the authentic Afro-Jamaican and the Japanese imitation becomes a circle more comfortably inclusive of Japanese subcultural practice' (Sterling 2010: 52).

This goes along with the discussion of what makes something Japanese, Jamaican, American, British or whatever country and culture you are discussing. I want to suggest that the music of Jamaica has distilled and dispersed throughout the world in a positive way that allows for people to represent the culture through sound. This does get difficult when discussing dress and religious incorporation to these subcultures and would benefit from a full-length discussion and book. For this work, these issues will be set a bit aside to look at how the sound itself was incorporated into a Japanese aesthetic. It is amazing that these countries are so far apart geographically and yet the sound of Jamaica influenced and created a subculture and eventually a cultural shift.

In Ian Condry's (2006) book, *Hip-Hop in Japan: Rap and the Paths of Cultural Globalization* is a discussion on these issues within the hip-hop community in Japan. He states: 'In this, I would argue, Japanese rappers, by allying themselves with African American rap, engage in what might be called a new cultural politics of affiliation' (Condry 2006: 29). This linkage is like the development and connection of dub in Japan, and the listeners and creators of reggae and dub music also engage in a 'new cultural politics of affiliation'. While doing so, the issues of appropriation still occur and remain for further discussion. 'Frequently songs by Japanese emcees outline histories of hip-hop in the United States and describe the Jamaican connections of DJs like Kool Herc and some other key pioneers such as Afrika Bambaataa and Grandmaster Flash' (Condry 2006: 33).

The arguments and discussions that involve hip-hop in Japan relate directly to those about reggae and dub. The cultural assimilation and deep knowledge of the Japanese participants encourage the outsider to look deeper than the initial imitation that occurs. Condry again suggests: 'First, it is important to recognize that in one sense Japanese hip-hop is, in fact, imitation' (2006: 34). He then goes on to discuss how this imitation is done with respect and deep understanding of the culture. For some, this imitation is flawed and extremely difficult due to issues of race, and these discussions can be linked with reggae and dub in Japan as well.

People in Japan, who were drawn to this subculture, began to blend the Jamaican style of reggae with Japanese effects and sound. The playing style was also very structured and more driven towards a type of perfection in the recording and performance of the material. This led to the harsher tones of Jamaica being cleaned up and focused a bit, but the feel remained. It is very interesting to listen to these first Japanese albums of dub and reggae for the similarities and differences in style and tone. In an interview with Dub-Stuy records, Hiroshi Takakura, founder of Riddim Chango Records, discussed Mute Beat stating:

> They used Jamaican reggae music as a platform, but they also had a definite Japanese identity. Because we don't have Caribbean musicians, the vibe and grooves are totally different from Jamaican reggae. Many reggae and dub bands in the early days were also influenced not only by reggae music but also jazz, hip-hop, etc. so the sounds of those bands are more diverse.
> (cited in Schenck 2019: n.pag.)

A similar shift occurred in England when the musicians began writing music to be dubbed instead of dubbing preexisting songs. What was once a way to reuse the song became a style all on its own.

This blending of styles is the important thing for this discussion. With Mute Beat, especially, Japanese song style and sounds blend with Jamaican rhythm and feel to create a distinctly Japanese dub. In other interviews, the first musicians to play reggae in Japan stated that they came from various different musical backgrounds. Many came from jazz groups or from studying music at school. Mostly, their first exposure to reggae was through playing it. This allowed for many different influences to impact the dub and reggae that was created in Japan.

The promotion group and label that influenced the reggae and dub scene the most from the beginning was Tachyon. Mavin Sterling (2011) also writes in 'Towards and analysis of global blackness: Race, representation, and jamaican popular culture in Japan':

> The scene developed in the 1980s under the influence of a number of entrepreneurial interests, including Overheat, which publishes the long-running Riddim magazine, and Tachyon, which published Reggae Magazine (no longer in publication). These companies also sponsored major reggae events in Japan, inviting Jamaican reggae acts to perform and record in the country, with moderate success.
>
> (2011: 10)

Tachyon folded in 1997 but started Japansplash and brought many performers and artists to the country. In 1995, the company promoted the release and signing, by Nippon Columbia, of a 10-year deal with Bunny Wailer to release Wailer's material. The releases were under the label name of Solomonic/Tuff Gong. Steve McClure states in *Billboard*: 'The first release is a 50-track, 2-CD collection of Wailer's remakes of classic Marley songs and is entitled "The Hall of Fame-A Tribute to Bob Marley's 50th Anniversary"' (1995: 41). This release demonstrated the importance of Bob Marley in Japan and how the music was promoted and sold.

Again, there are two strains of listening and performance styles in Japan, dance hall and dub. 'Dub-based sound systems share the musical manipulation and MC orality of dancehall even as they tend to retain more of roots reggae's Rasta-influenced message of spiritual uplift' (Sterling 2010: 65). These dub-based sound systems are the focus for this work. It also becomes interesting when discussing dub that, as Sterling states again: 'It is hard to find anyone deeply involved in any aspect of Jamaican culture in Japan who is not also a musician' (2010: 65). The distillation of sound occurs when the musicians take the music of Jamaica and reformat it with Japanese sounds and feel. The most well-known example of this is Mute Beat.

Mute Beat began when Kazumi 'Echo' Kodama, trumpet player, Hideyuki Imai, drummer and Takayoshi Matsunaga, bassist went into a studio, Studio Abo, to experiment. The band grew to consist of piano, drums, bass, trumpet and trombone. They first released a 10-inch single on Pithecan Records in 1983. The A-side 'Butterfly' is a vocal duet, while the B-side is the first recording of 'Still Echo' that was released. The full-length titled *Still Echo* was released on Wackie's in 1986. The group is also an integral part of this discussion as they, like Matumbi, focused on live dub and incorporated an engineer to dub the band live. Izumi 'Dub Master X' Miyazaki became an integral part of Mute Beat's sound and show.

DMX's sound can be heard on Mute Beat's *Mute Beat Dubwise*, which is a pure dub record featuring DMX, Lee 'Scratch' Perry and a King Tubby apprentice, Ken 'Fatman' Gordon. This record was partially mixed at Tuff Gong studio in Jamaica and at Bullwackie's studio in New York where they added the vocal parts. It is a perfect example of the engineer being the focus of the sound. This record, in 1989, showcased what was possible in Japan and in the rest of the world, with dub music and the distillation of sound. The combination is a direct representation of how dub has crossed cultural barriers and found a home throughout the world.

Mute Beat also gives rise to the discussion about the incorporation of Jamaican music into new countries. They took the style and bass-driven sound of Jamaica and added Japanese aesthetics and sounds to the songs and performance. This created a new sound in dub and, like African Head Charge and some of the other developments in England led by Adrian Sherwood, shifted what people consider dub today. The incorporation of Japanese sounds led Mute Beat to become very popular in Japan as they were not copying a Jamaican sound or style but using it to influence their own creations. This influence can be heard on all of their recordings, but the focus here will be on their full-length release on the Overheat and Wackie's label, *Still Echo*.

This full length was the first full length to be released by the band in 1987 in Japan on Overheat Records and then was re-released in 1993 and 2011 on Wackie's. The musicians on this record are Kazumi Kodama, trumpet; Akihito Masui, trombone; Hirofumi Asamoto, keyboards; Gota Yashiki, Hideyuki Imai, drums and percussion; Takayoshi Matsunaga, bass; and it was mixed by Izumi 'DMX' Miyazaki. The tracklist for the original release on Overheat records is 1, 'Coffia'; 2, 'Organ's Melody'; 3, 'Echo's Song'; 4, 'Summertime-Frozen Sun'; 5, 'After the Rain'; 6, 'No Problem'; 7, 'Still Echo' and 8, 'Still Echo (melodica Mix)'. The vinyl release on Wackie's is slightly different: A1 'After the Rain', A2 'Coffia', A3 'Organ's Melody', A4 'Echo's Song', B1 'Summertime-Frozen Sun', B2 'No Problem' and B3 'Still Echo'. For this discussion, we will follow the original release.

Timbre 9

The overall timbre of this record is more towards a ska or reggae release as the trumpet carries each track. This makes the songs brighter than other dub records in this discussion. These are also all songs that are played and slightly manipulated by 'DMX,' creating songs to be dubbed live or in later studio releases. This record is aligned more with Prince Buster's *The Message Dubwise* in this aspect. There are effects throughout the songs, but they are minimal to let the instrumental form take shape. This is also a record with songs that are mostly set up in a jazz format where the head melody is played, and then a solo section takes place and then the head comes back in at the end of the song.

These small shifts in writing demonstrate the ways in which the Japanese aesthetic comes through into the Jamaican rhythm. While the feel of Jamaica is there, the clean sound and jazz format link this record with a newer sound. Much like the dub that was created in England, this record was written to be dubbed. It is extremely interesting that the original sounds of dub were influenced by the jazz formats that occurred in ska. This is reasserted here in the structure of the song and in the focus on the trumpet. What may be considered, stereotypically, as 'Japanese sounds', are not here. But the playing style and structure show a distinct take on Jamaican music.

This record is also an example of what people consider dub in Japan. This is not the steppers beat or a lover's rock feel that is so popular in the dance halls and with sound systems. This is an album that is meant to be listened to for its musicality and insertion by the engineer. These insertions, generally, are with a delay, but the effects used differ in some parts. Listening to this record is similar to listening to a record of the Skatalites being dubbed by a different engineer.

'Coffia', 1, demonstrates this jazz format precisely and begins the album with an upbeat ska song that shows the trumpet and trombone player's timbre and playing ability. The drums on the track are also ska in tempo and playing style, while the mixing and effects come in and out throughout the track, they are minimal compared with other engineers in this discussion.

The track begins with a syncopated opening and then kicks into the horn line, which consists of an A section and a B section. The main melody is carried by the trumpet and trombone, while the bass and drums play a driving pattern. When the B section comes in, the organ is mixed higher, and the first full delay on the trumpet comes in at the end of the B section. After the initial head of the melody, there is a small transition section that features a keyboard line and then the song breaks into a solo section beginning with the trombone and followed by a trumpet solo.

What is most interesting about the timbre of this song is the bass line, which is played on an upright bass and in close to the same pattern throughout the entire song. The bass is toned fairly high in this genre of music as well and mixed at the top of the mix. The transition keyboard part comes in after the solo section and then the head is brought back into the song, but this time is mixed by 'DMX' to add delay and effects to the melody. The snare hit is affected by a large reverb, and the horn line is pushed through a delay. The bass is also dropped out of this section in the beginning to let the horn line carry the song. It then comes in after the initial line to begin the second occurrence of the A section horn line.

The song ends after the B section with the transition keyboard line and hits from the horns. It drives to the end with the darkest timbre of the song in the keyboard and ends with a delayed horn hit.

'Organ's Melody', 2, starts with a darker timbre and slower pace. Here, the drums are effected, and the horn line is accented by keyboard lines and hits. The main melody is over a more reggae centred drum line as well. The structure of this song is set up with the A section of the melody being repeated after the intro. This repetition begins with the trumpet alone and then is joined by the trombone to carry through the B section of the song. Then the A section is repeated again. After this, the song has the intro section again before going to a dubbed out solo section.

This dubbed out section, starting at 2:31, is most related to the darker timbre in dub as the bass is mixed almost to the point of distortion in points and the bass and drums carry the rhythm while the keyboard chomps along for the rhythmic interplay. The drums have the most effects on them in this section as the fills are digitised. At 3:41, the trumpet comes in again with a horn line that is delayed, and this is followed by organ swells that lead back to the head of the song.

Rhythmic interplay 9

'Echo's Song', 3, is a heavily syncopated song in the drum part and begins with a drum pattern with the trumpet playing the lead melody and the trombone playing a counter melody. The rhythmic interplay is carried by the organ and drums here as the bass line rolls through the hits on the drums. This song has a type of broken beat where the listener is grooving but trying to find the flow. The rhythmic interplay is what creates this flow and the trumpet line carries the song forward.

It is also interesting that this song has minimal effects, other than some small reverb on the horns. In the solo section, the trumpet is played with a Harmon mute in it which adds to the strangeness of the song's timbre and feel. Then the trombone solo is played with delay on the short hits of the part. This followed by the trumpet melody coming in on its own with no bass line, countered by the trombone line.

The bass line comes in during the B section of the melody and the song ends with the melody and counter being played over the syncopated drums. These drums relate slightly to a burru beat but this song highlights the fragmented writing of the band and how they were adept at building grooves out of angular melody lines over an interesting and original beat pattern.

'Summertime – Frozen Sun', 4, is a cover of a jazz standard and opens with an organ run with the trumpet coming in with a flourish over the organ chords. These are both without effects and the head of the song ends with the trumpet carrying the melody out. The song shifts to a hard-driving reggae beat at 1:56 with a drum hit.

This is where the rhythmic interplay occurs in the keyboard chomp, while the drums are put through effects. The bass line is pushed in the mix as well but not affected. The trumpet plays the main melody of the song as the keyboard keeps the upbeat rhythmic interplay of the song. There is also some percussion in the main section as the trumpet solo is played with delay and is sporadic and spacey.

At 3:59, the delay is used on the keyboard to set up a drop of all of the instruments except the bass, this time with reverb, until 4:21 where the trumpet comes in again, but this time there are effects on the drums and a patched in spacy samples with the main rhythm.

The rhythmic interplay through this dub section is carried with the bass line and the drums and then the organ comes back into accent the part.

At 6:00, the trumpet plays a falling line that leads into an even heavier dub section. Throughout this, the keyboard carried the rhythmic interplay and allows the rest of the instruments the space to play. The trumpet comes in and out with delayed lines while the bass drives the rhythm. DMX adds in effected samples and reverb on the drum hits, while the trumpet carries the song to end with the organ syncopating then holding as samples are used again.

Re-production 9
The re-production of tracks for this record is very interesting and is displayed in 'After the Rain', 5, as a drum machine starts the song and is accented with 1980s drum machine hits. The bass comes in with the drum machine, and then the melody is played on a keyboard while the rhythmic interplay of the song is played by a keyboard chomp. This is an electronic track that has a darker timbre, but the re-production is fully done in a studio.

The drum line is constant throughout the song while the keyboard swells in parts and the bass line carries the song. This is an electronic song with an acoustic bass. This re-production is relevant here as the keyboard parts swell back and forth and play with the bass line creating the song. While the melody is played on the keyboard, it is the bass line that has the most interesting part in this song. The constant drum machine part allows for the bass to move more than in other songs and the song ends with the bass and drum machine only.

The next track, 'No Problem', 6, is a funk song that is constructed to groove and begins with horn and drum hits before breaking into the groove. The song follows the same format with an A section followed by a B Section and then repeated as the melody twice before going into a bridge section that leads back to the melody. The way that the piano comes in between the horn line is interesting as well here. The percussion also adds to the funk of this mix and drums and bass play with the band as a tight unit.

The song begins a breakdown part at 3:20 with samples being played over the drum pattern. This is the constructive element as the song breaks into a New Orleans style funk song, while the percussion drives the beat. The different instruments begin a solo jam that has the trumpet and trombone playing back and forth with each other as the keyboard, bass and drums carry the groove. This is not a dub track in any way but carries dub elements with it. What this track does demonstrate, again, is the musicianship of the band and how they could play in many different styles. After this breakdown, the song comes back to the head. The song ends with the breakdown section again and the drums and percussion only.

The next song on this release is the band's hit song and the title track of the record, 'Still Echo'. This was originally recorded as a single before this release and gave the band its fame in the Japanese scene. It is a song that resonates with dub effects, a grooving drum line and a strong dark bass line. The song opens with a horn flourish over this drum and bass pattern, while the keyboard syncopates the track. There are many interesting things in the writing of this track as the bass line counters the horns. The trombone part is also playing a counter melody with the trumpet.

The mixing of this version is also interesting as the hits on the snare drum are affected, and the bass is pushed to the top of the mix. The melody gives way to a keyboard swell to allow for the dub feel in the bass and drums to ride for a bit, then the horn line comes back again. Once the main melody section is played, the song breaks into a dub section.

Here the chords modulate slightly, and the bass drives the groove with the keyboard chomping and the drums playing the consistent drum pattern while DMX adds effects to them. The trumpet comes back in for some short-delayed patterns as well. The song then has keyboard swells that lead back to the melody line in the horns. The keyboard swells are used throughout the song to set up the melody line and to add to the constructive element of the track. The song ends with the main melody line being played over these keyboard swells and the horns are delayed on the last note.

The last song is a version, 'Still Echo (melodica mix)' which has Augustus Pablo playing melodica over a slightly different version of the song. Most strikingly is the drum patter that changes to a one-drop pattern. The effects are also used much more here, and the melodica is the main element in the song, instead of the trumpet. After the intro drum hit the song begins with melodica and then builds from there.

The re-production of this track is paramount as it allows Pablo to play in and out of the main melody while the drum part shifts to a more standard reggae beat. The bass is also at the top of the mix while the organ bubbles throughout the song. All of this gives Pablo the ability to come in and out of the mix with the melodica and you hear many interesting melodica patterns throughout the song, switching from chorded phrases to single-note lines and flourishes. The main melody comes back in the middle of the song here and then the song dissolves into a full dub with the melodica carrying out to the end.

In an interview with David Katz on this recording, which happened when Augustus Pablo was in Japan for Japan Splash 86: "'At the beginning he didn't look too enthusiastic,' says DMX of Pablo, "but after he listened to the sound of it, he seemed to be motivated to play'" (Katz 2014b: n.pag). This version spiked the popularity of the group and led to more recordings and live shows, including support for famous Jamaican musicians.

Completion 8

The sound of Jamaica came to Japan in a way that was similar to other parts of the world. What is interesting is how the Japanese took the sound and made it a part of their own culture. The two countries differ in style and feel so much that the sound of reggae transferring, and distilling is extremely interesting. What made this sound so important to the Japanese people? Why did they take to this style of music so completely? These are questions for an anthropologist to take on and some have already. Groups like Mute Beat represent key elements in the distillation of sound to Japan. Through the combination of Jamaican tone and style, and Japanese musicality and formal use of structure, the music becomes extremely interesting and complex.

Mute Beat frames this discussion as they embody the Japanese aesthetic mixed with the Jamaican feel and sound. Listening to their music is enthralling and opens up the representations and links to other distillations. The songs are more akin to the songs of Adrian Sherwood and On-U Sound releases or Mad Professor and Dennis Bovell's work. The album demonstrates that the raw and more simplistic tones and songs from Jamaica can carry throughout the world. Even through the manipulation of different label heads and producers, the style and sound of Jamaica still carries through.

This also occurred when reggae and dub distilled in England. The sound changes and shifts to become more 'British' in ways that have already been discussed. Throughout the world, Jamaican music has influenced people in this way, and many different cultures have blended it with their own. The tone, feel, playing style and structure of Jamaican music can be seen throughout the world, and, in Japan, this distillation joins the Japanese aesthetic in very interesting ways. Here we can hear the combination and the development of culture within a culture that is discussed by Erlmann and others when they suggest that sound can create and dominate cultural changes.

Dub works within many different cultures all around the world and the small representation of examples in this chapter only start this conversation. It is important to not just stop at Mute Beat for this discussion, as there are many other groups and more contemporary artists in Japan doing this. The key points of discussion also carry through to these groups, and it becomes extremely interesting when looking at Americans, like Jeremy Freeman, of Deadly Dragon Sound, who transplanted to Japan and became a successful DJ there, as well. All of these conversations start with the sound of dub and reggae music and how it has transformed and shifted throughout the world.

Today, Japan is still on top when it comes to dance hall and sound system style. Mighty Crown continues to wow crowds and win sound clashes throughout the world and Junko and others continue to take home the title of Dancehall queen. The issues that arise about whether this is good or bad for Jamaica come up often and are important to discuss but for this chapter and book the sound is the key. The sound of Jamaica influenced an entire culture thousands of miles away.

Chapter 9
Distillation of Sound

You have to immerse yourself slowly –
　　　　　　　　Neil Fraser (aka Mad Professor) (2018)

Figure 9.1: Part of King Jammy's sound system. Photo: Courtesy of Cassandra Abbey (2019).

The culture of dub developed out of the technology that became available to Jamaica. The mixing board and two-track reel-to-reel recorders made it possible to manipulate and change the existing tracks in a way that changed the way people listen to music. The people who were using and working on these machines shifted the way that the music was heard and created a new language that spread throughout the world. Engineers and producers became prominent in the creation of music because of the culture of dub, and this has lasted to contemporary times. The genre began with rhythm tracks being reused and quickly shifted to the dub genre with King Tubby and others becoming creative artists through the technology available. The debate over what dub is continues with today's producers, but the culture that was created in the studio is not up for debate. While some people claim dub began with specials, voicing over tracks for a sound system, others stick to the definitions and genres given here. The culture of dub relates to the technological shift that occurred in music because of the engineers and producers.

From the first version-driven dubs *Java, Java, Java, Java* and *Aquarius Dub* to the dub albums full of creative influence *King Tubbys Meets Rockers Uptown* and *Blackboard Jungle Dub*, the culture of dub was formed. It was then spread to the world with Prince Buster's *The Message Dubwise* and the lead single from *King Tubbys Meets the Rockers Uptown*. As the genre spread, it quickly changed again with the influence of new technology to the island and the digital revolution started. When dub began the shift was so rapid on the island that many things got lost. Mad Professor states: 'The speed of transitions caused a lack of understanding' (Fraser 2018).

Mad Professor discussed this lack of understanding and stated that the first reception of dub on the island was as scary and unwelcome music only fit for ganja smokers (Fraser 2018). It took the sound systems playing the tracks consistently to gain any reputation or respect outside of the yard. Many producers also lacked an understanding that the music must be correct and recorded by outstanding musicians for the dub to come off well. In discussing the influence of technology on dub from the beginning to today Mad Professor states: 'People have got to understand quality and where it's coming from' (Fraser 2018). He stated that his start to dub was when a James Brown and His Famous Flames record landed in Jamaica as 'Part B', which was an instrumental version of the hit song 'Try Me'. This is a strange statement as the B-side to 'Try Me' is 'Tell Me What I Did Wrong', but nostalgia and memory are often faulty.

In many ways, Jamaican music is rooted in American blues, r&b and swing. Dub is no different, as the instrumental versions of popular American songs were the first to be voiced over in the sound systems. From there, the music grew and developed into its own art form when technology became available. To Mad Professor, Prince Buster's *The Message Dubwise* was the first dub album as it crossed borders and influenced the world. The influence continues in today's dub culture.

There is a large culture founded on the concepts and manipulations of the original dub artists in the world today. Sound system culture continues to grow with multiple systems throughout the world competing every year for the title of champion. Reggae Sumfest, a festival owned by Josef Bogdanovich, features a battle between sound systems every year. This festival is highly attended and one of the most important events in Jamaica from a tourist standpoint. This week-long celebration of all styles of Jamaican music began in 1993 with Founders Summerfest Productions Limited and is now owned by Down sound Records.

Reggae Sumfest was started after Sunsplash left Montego Bay for Ocho Rios. The community and business owners in Montego Bay knew they had to fill the space that was left and started their own festival. With the momentum that Sunsplash had started throughout the world, Reggae Sumfest began and carried on the tradition of a week-long festival in Montego Bay. Both of these festivals were influential in the distillation of sound from Jamaica as tourists from all over the world still come to celebrate Jamaican music.

The spread of dub culture has created many discussions about the history and importance of Jamaican music as the Japanese have been the largest purveyors of dub in recent times. Mighty Crown, a Japanese sound system led by Masta Simon, Sammi T and Ninja, won the 2018 world clash at Reggae Sumfest defeating Tony Matterhorn. This demonstrates how far the culture of dub has traveled after the first cultural immersions happened in England.

The single that was pressed with 'King Tubbys Meets the Rockers Uptown' on the A-side was played in 1977 on Tommy Vance's show on the BBC. On 16 July 1977, Johnny Rotten was being interviewed about the Sex Pistols album *Never Mind the Bollocks* and decided to end the formal interview and just play his favorite records. He played the single 'King Tubby Meets the Rockers Uptown' and the influence of dub music took over England. Alex Young (2008) talks about this moment in 'Dusting them off: Augustus Pablo-King Tubby meets rockers uptown' and states: 'Suddenly, unsuspecting punks were being spoon-fed prime-cut dub by the ringleader of their own revolution. The deep, cavernous sound of "King Tubby Meets Rockers Uptown" became the hallmark of bands immediately to come' (n.pag.). The culture of dub influenced the world from this point on.

The Message Dubwise had been released in 1972 and had introduced dub to England but the lead punk of the time spinning a track broke the mold, and from then on, everyone was on a quest to find and listen to dub music. This is the distillation of sound that began in Jamaica when the engineers and producers gained popularity. The technology allowed this to happen, and through this, the people became famous for what they did behind a mixing console. The timbre, rhythmic interplay and re-production that created dub culture are still a part of contemporary music and gaining more attention each day.

In New York groups such as Subatomic Soundsystem, Dub Stuy, Federation Sound, Dub is a Weapon, Easy Star Records, Crazy Baldhead, Tiklah, Soon Come and many others continue to create and promote dub and reggae music. Max Glazer, of Federation Sound, champions contemporary reggae music as a DJ on Red Bull Radio and toured opening for Lee 'Scratch' Perry and Subatomic Soundsystem. These contemporary groups are not only in NYC but spread all over the globe. Noah Shachtman and Emch started Subatomic Sound in 1999 and Dub Stuy began in 2012 when Quoc Pham and Jay Spaker met up in the Bed Stuy area of Brooklyn.

In England, labels like Nice Up, Bokeh Versions and many others carry dub into the future as it blends with dubstep and grime. Nice Up and Bokeh each fixate on the older sounds of dub. In Japan, there are many labels featuring dub with Dub Store selling Jamaican releases and Fishmans performing dub since 1987.

In Jamaica, there are still many sound systems playing reggae and dub live in the dance hall. Stone Love continues to pack the dance hall whenever they play and Jam One and selectors Pink Panther and Ricky Trooper continue to draw crowds. In Jamaica, every night of the week is a dance-hall party. Mojito Mondays and Uptown Mondays, Boasy Tuesday, Stone Love hosts Weddy Weddy Wednesdays, Whopping Thursdays and many events on the weekend all provide the soundtrack to Jamaican culture. The music in the dance hall has shifted, but the timbre that began with dub is still dominant.

The sound of these albums has created and influenced a culture surrounding them that continues to change and affect the world. This sound, determined through technology, not only influenced culture but also the way that music is created, mixed and produced. There are many people today that still utilise dub mixing techniques in contemporary music of all genres. A certain bass tone, the way a bass drum sounds, the rhythmic interplay of the guitar and piano, all can be heard in popular music today. The engineer's use of reverb, delay and high- and low-pass filters is still creating sounds that started in Jamaica, and the mixing board is now viewed as an instrument where engineers craft the mix.

The original producers and engineers like Errol Thompson, Sylvan Morris, Carlton Lee, Herman Chin-Loy, Clive Chin and others took tracks of existing music and reused them to produce something new for the sound system audience. These new collections of songs broke the way that people were used to hearing music by pulling out and pushing in different areas of the song. Creating a depth to the music by removing parts became a signature of dub and then the addition of new sounds would come later. Tracks like 'Guiding Dub', 'Jah Rock' and 'I Man' all demonstrate the ways in which timbre and rhythmic interplay can be achieved by directly removing parts of the original track. This continued with the creative force of the engineers.

Lee 'Scratch' Perry and King Tubby created dub through their additions and manipulations of the tracks. The timbre and rhythmic interplay are still present in these albums, but the re-production of the music is where the dub begins. Perry's additions of sounds into the mix, with King Tubby as the engineer, created the biggest shift of what dub music was and still is. Songs like 'Mooving Skank' and 'Kaya Skank' show the insertions and methods of re-production that Perry used with Tubby at the

Figure 9.2: Mural on Orange Street, Kingston, JA. Photo: Courtesy of Cassandra Abbey (2019).

controls. While the other two albums formed the basis of the version genre, *Blackboard Jungle Dub* stands as an example of dub for its creativity and re-production of tracks.

King Tubbys Meets the Rockers Uptown began the entire culture of dub through the manipulations of technology. Creating a studio and vocal booth in a small house and changing the mixing board to suit his purposes, Tubby created what most people consider the dub genre. His studio became known as the place to get versions and his re-production solidified dub throughout the world. With his single and Prince Buster's *The Message Dubwise*, dub was spread throughout England and to the rest of the world. Buster's album bridges the gap between version and dub genres as his popularity led the way for these dubs. The creation of the culture of dub stems from these five albums and begins the story of technology influencing music.

When reggae and dub get to New York City the influence shifts and becomes less direct but more pronounced in feel. With the concepts learned from sound system culture and dub music, Kool

Herc and others started what would go on to become hip hop and rap. The manipulation of sonic frequencies and the use of records and turntables as tools and musical instruments created an entire new genre of music. While this was occurring, Lloyd Barnes and others brought Jamaican music to New York and the culture of reggae and dub took hold.

Clocktower, VP Records and places like Jammyland and Ernie B's continued the tradition of Jamaican music and helped to expose many people to dub and reggae. The distillation of sound in New York also began the shift to Japan and other parts of the world. Wackie's is still looked at as a foundation label for dub and reggae music, and VP continues to shape what reggae is in contemporary times.

From New York City and Jamaica, the music and culture of dub and reggae reached Japan. Here the distillation takes on a distinct shape when Japanese aesthetic and fell blends with Jamaican music. The sound system culture took over in Japan, and dub was relegated to a musician's type of music. This gave bands and engineers the opportunity in the studio to produce dub that related more to the original versions heard in Jamaica. Mute Beat and other groups took the feel of reggae and put their Japanese feel and structure to it. Mighty Crown sound system and other DJs and selectors continue to make Japan one of the largest places for reggae music in the world.

For the dub engineer, the way the machine was used and controlled was extremely important. The connection between the engineer and the mixing desk was utilised like the musician and his or her instrument. This forced the music and sound into new territory and created a different dimension of listening. In *The Audible Past: Cultural Origins of Sound Reproduction*, Jonathan Sterne (2003) states: 'The very possibility of sound reproduction emerges from the character and connectedness of the medium' (225). You can hear the manipulation of the original sound. The destruction of the voice, the splitting of the track and the addition of sounds that were theirs and not the musicians.

The biggest change in technology that occurred in Jamaica was the introduction of the reel-to-reel tape machine. Along with this came the MCI mixing board, and together these machines changed how we hear music. Dub was not just about the removal of vocals to give the DJ something to chat over, it was about what was done to the track through the mixing board and tape machine. Dub also represents the darker side of Jamaican culture through the timbre and fixation on the bass and drums.

The political changes that happened in the mid-1970s in Jamaica were heard in the music and timbre of the tracks of dub. The dark tones resonated with the lower classes and became 'scary' to other listeners. The dance hall shifted to reflect these dark tones, and the sound of the street was created through dub. As the oil crisis hit and the political parties were at war, the people responded through music and dance. The culture of dub began this response. Even in songs without vocals, the darker feel of the streets and the anger and fear of the people was heard through dub. A simple listen to the ska of the 1960s and the dub of the 1970s demonstrates this shift in timbre and feel.

Producers like Lee 'Scratch' Perry delivered their artistic statement through dub and the people behind the mixing board gained a reputation as artists through dub. Taking the atoms of the music and changing them to reflect, the engineer was the key development in dub and its culture. Perry and King Tubby reflect this in every track of sound. Both deconstruct music to the atomic level and rebuild it with their influence and creative focus. Dub is about replication and what is changed when doing so. Taking the track and creating something new with existing parts is what dub is. Perry and Tubby demonstrated the ways in which this can be a creative process more than just one for consumer consumption.

This destructive technique is what allows for dub to take prominence in a culture of rapid expansion. Dub places a distinct emphasis on sound and, through technology, recreates the song into something much more. When listening to a dub track, you are exposed to many different sound structures that appear on successive hearings. In a discussion on the way Dub 'infects' the listeners Steve Goodman (2010) in *Sonic Warfare* states:

> The 'dub virus' relates not just to the direct influence of the dub reggae sound on other musics, but more than this, its catalysis of an abstract sound machine revolving around the studio as instrument and the migration of a number of production and playback processes.
>
> (159)

These processes define the ways in which the engineer destroyed the track and then recreated and added their own voice to the mix.

Dub is also groove music that acts to prove the continuity of time and fixates us on the ways in which we exist in a culture. For popular music listeners, Prince Buster's *The Message Dubwise* acted as a demonstration of dub that could become popular. This allowed the music to spread to the rest of the world and created a path for Jamaican dub that is still being followed today. While dub tracks play with the timing of the music in the use of delay and reverb, the duration of time is proven through listening to each sound. This creates a heard existence that differs from other music genres and captures the listener in different ways.

These different ways are paths to attunement in the listener. The acoustic space of the song is delivered in the dubbing of each track. The point of dub lies in getting to the basis of the music and connecting the person to the feel of the song. The space within the track is determined through the engineer's use of the melody and the different ways of manipulating the track with reverb and delay. This emptiness then allows the listener to attune to the music through tone and feel. This emptiness can be heard on 'Jah Rock' and 'Rumbo Malt' from *Aquarius Dub* and many others. For dub, the manipulation of the track is the key to the shift in sound. According to Kodo Eshun (1998) in *More Brilliant than the Sun*: 'When you sculpt space with the mixing deck, these technical effects – gate and reverb, echo and flange – are routes through a network of volumes, doorways and tunnels connecting spatial architectures' (63).

These albums, specifically, open the discussion on the importance of the engineer and producer in dub music. The way that the original track has been manipulated signifies the presence of someone other than the musicians on the track. Even though the main melody line is distinguishable, it has been rendered through a delay processor. The echo that this creates is not possible with an instrument alone and mandates that the audience pay attention to the feel and effect that the engineer has placed on the track. These engineers and producers had extremely limited technological apparatus compared to today's studios and were able to insert their presence into the track with only a mixing console, two-track recorder and home-built effects.

The development of the record player, reel-to-reel tape recorder and the mixing console led to the producer and engineer gaining focus and becoming stars within Jamaican music. Dub music was created through the destruction and reformation of the track to 'play' the mixing console as an instrument. Erik Davis (2008) in '"Roots and Wire" remix' states: 'strip the music down to the bare bones of drum and bass and then build it up again through layers of distortion, percussive noise, and electronic ectoplasm' (63). The result is the presence of the engineer and producer within Jamaican music and culture through technology. This music opens many lines of thought and encourages multiple readings on technological uniqueness in our non-auratic society.

The sound has been distilled and reformatted through the technology that was available at the time. With this, distillation came the ability of the culture of dub to form and be delivered throughout the world. By taking the basic tracks of the song and shifting them creatively, the engineers and producers of these albums formed a culture that continues to resonate. Through looking closely at dub, we can attempt to explore and understand

Figure 9.3: Dave the Dub Cat in Jammyland. Photo: Courtesy of Ira Heaps.

how technological development plays a role in creation. This writing seeks to begin the discussion into the qualities of uniqueness and live-ness that are produced within Dub and how these qualities continue through society. The distinct nature of dub within the sound system culture and dance halls created a place for the engineer and producer to gain notice and the technology used was responsible for this occurrence.

Endnotes

1. Sound systems were outdoor stacks of speakers that, at first, were owned by liquor store owners and used as a way to get people to buy liquor. These systems were set up outside, usually in a lot, and acted as a community gathering point and avenue for news as well.
2. The term 'riddim' is Jamaican slang for the music of the song without the entire vocal track. This term is used differently by different people at different times, but here it is used to discuss the song without the entire vocal track.
3. The author's transcription does not attempt to transcribe the patois, but instead renders what was said into standard English.
4. Slack songs are popular songs that have lewd lyrics sung over the original rhythm track.

References

Abel, Mark (2016), *Groove: An Aesthetic of Measured Time*, Chicago: Haymarket Books.

Adorno, Theodor W. (1941), 'The radio symphony: An experiment in theory', in P. F. Lazerfeld and Frank N. Stanton (eds), *Radio Research*, New York: Duell, Sloan and Pearce.

Adorno, Theodor W. and Thomas Y. Levin (1990), 'The form of the phonograph record', *October*, Winter, pp. 48–55.

Agyekum, Seba Kwesi Damani (2018), 'A history of hip hop in perspective', Academia, https://www.academia.edu/12545353/A_History_of_Hip_Hop_in_Perspective 3. Accessed 6 June 2018

Albini, Steve (1993), 'The problem with music', *The Baffler*, 5 December, https://thebaffler.com/salvos/the-problem-with-music. Accessed 21 October 2018.

Ali, Sultan (2018), personal interview, Detroit, 11 April.

Anon. (2008), 'Icon–King Tubby reigns', *Jamaica Gleaner*, 25 March, http://old.jamaica-gleaner.com/gleaner/20080325/ent/ent4.html. Accessed 25 January 2019.

Anon. (2019a), 'History', VP Records, https://www.vprecords.com/history/. Accessed 3 March 2020

Anon. (2019b), 'A reggae music journey', https://www.vprecords.com/a-reggae-journey/. Accessed 3 March 2020.

Ascott, Roy (2000), *Art, Technology, Consciousness: Mind @ Large*, Bristol: Intellect.

Attali, Jacques (1985), *Noise: The Political Economy of Music*, Minneapolis: University of Minnesota Press.

Augustyn, Heather (2010), *Ska: An Oral History*, Jefferson: McFarland & Co.

Bachelard, Gaston (2000), *The Dialectic of Duration*, Lanham, ML: Rowman & Littlefield.

Bennett, Matthew (2014), 'Dubplate culture: Analogue islands in the digital stream', *Red Bull Music Academy*, 30 October, http://daily.redbullmusicacademy.com/2014/10/dubplate-culture-feature. Accessed 25 January 2019.

Best, Curwen (2004), *Culture @ the Cutting Edge: Tracking Caribbean Popular Music*, Kingston: University of the West Indies Press.

Black, Roy (2011), 'The music of politics: Popular songs campaign hits '70s peak', *Jamaica Gleaner*, 25 December, http://jamaicagleaner.com/gleaner/20111225/ent/ent10.html. Accessed 15 December 2018

Bonitto, Brian (2012), 'King Tubby, the sound creator', *Jamaica Observer*, 7 June, http://www.jamaicaobserver.com/entertainment/King-Tubby--the-sound-creator_11886528. Accessed 25 January 2019.

Bovell, Dennis (2019), personal interview, Holton Heath, Poole, UK, 11 October.

Bradley, Lloyd (2000), *Bass Culture: When Reggae Was King*, London: Penguin.

Brenner, Dan (2020), personal interview, Detroit, 15 April.

Broughton, Frank (2018), 'From the DJ history archives: Frank Broughton takes a walk around the Bronx with a true hip-hop pioneer', *Red Bull Music Academy*, http://daily.redbullmusicacademy.com/2018/01/kool-herc-interview. Accessed 8 June 2019.

Brown, Hopeton Overton (2019), personal interview, Detroit, 13 December.

Buckley, Roy (2015), 'The greatest record shop in the world', *Deadly Dragon Sounds*, https://deadlydragonsounds.blogspot.com/search?q=the+greatest+record+shop. Accessed 1 March 2018.

Buknor, Michael and Donnell, Allison (2011), 'Dub poetry as postmodern art form: Self-conscious of critical reception', *The Routledge Companion to Anglophone Caribbean Literature*, London and New York: Routledge, pp. 255–65.

The BullWackie's All Stars ([1975] 2007), *Free for All*, New York and Germany: Wackie's/Aries.

Burgess, Richard James (2014), *The History of Music Production*, Oxford: Oxford Univesity Press.

Chin, Clive (2003), 'Clive Chin', interview, Red Bull Music Academy, https://static1.squarespace.com/static/58763ec0c534a5e7e2b65fe2/t/5b-d57888ec212d4d8804b0cf/1540716683666/Popular+inquiry_Vol2_Sokei.pdf. Accessed 20 January 2019.

Chude-Sokei, Louis (2018), 'Dr. Satan's Echo Chamber: Reggae, technology, and the diaspora process', *The Journal of Kitsch, Camp, and Mass Culture*, 1, https://static1.squarespace.com/static/58763ec0c534a5e7e2b65fe2/t/5bd57888ec212d4d8804b0cf/1540716683666/Popular+inquiry_Vol2_Sokei.pdf. Accessed 18 June 2021.

Clarke, Augustus 'Guisse' (O.D.) (2018), personal interview, Detroit, 2 October.

Collingwood, Jeremy (2010), *Lee 'Scratch' Perry: Kiss Me Neck: The Scratch Story in Words, Pictures, and Records*, London: Cherry Red Books.

Condry, Ian (2006), *Hip-Hop in Japan: Rap and the Paths of Cultural Globalization*, Durham and London: Duke University Press.

Cooper, Stephen (2018), 'Interview with Scientist – Part2', http://reggaevibes.com/articles/2019/02/interview-with-scientist-part-2. Accessed 30 December 2018 [no longer available].

Cumming, Tim (2006), 'Dennis Bovell: The dub master', *Independent*, https://www.independent.co.uk/arts-entertainment/music/features/dennis-bovell-the-dub-master-6105037.html. Accessed 25 November 2019.

Cunningham, Janine Elizabeth (2019), 'Jah 9', *Dub Conference*, panel discussion, University of the West Indies, Kingston, JA, 15 February.

Davis, Erik (2008), '"Roots and Wires" remix: Polyrhythmic tricks the black electronic', *Sound Unbound: Sampling Digital Music and Culture*, Cambridge, Paul Miller, MA: MIT pp. 53–72.

Davis, Stephen (1976), 'Fear in paradise', *New York Times*, 25 July, https://www.nytimes.com/1976/07/25/archives/fear-in-paradise-the-real-jamaica-is-an-angry-state-locked-in-a.html. Accessed 8 July 2018.

Eco, Umberto (1984), *Semiotics and the Philosophy of Language*, Indiana University Press: Bloomington.

Ehrengardt, Thibault (2020), *King Tubbys: The Dub Master*, France: Dread Editions.

Erlmann, Veit (2004), *Hearing Cultures: Essays on Sound, Listening, and Modernity*, Oxford: Berg.

Eshun, Kodwo (1998), *More Brilliant than the Sun: Adventures in Sonic Fiction*, London: Quartet.

Fraser, Neil (2018), personal interview, Detroit, 1 November.

Frith, Simon (1987), 'Towards an aesthetic of popular music', in R. D. Leppert and S. McClary (eds), *Music and Society: The Politics of Composition, Performance, and Reception*, Cambridge: Cambridge University Press.

Frith, Simon (1996), *Performing Rites: On the Value of Popular Music*, Cambridge, MA: Harvard University Press.

Gooden, Lou (2015), *Dancehall Sound System: The Good, The Bad and the Ugliest*, vol. 1, Kentucky: Create Space Publishers.

Goodman, Steve (2010), *Sonic Warfare: Sound, Affect, and the Ecology of Fear*, Cambridge, MA: MIT Press.

Hagerman, Brent (2015), 'From dub plate to dancehall: Versioning as an analogue template for digital reggae', in D.P. Hope (ed.), *Reggae From Yaad: Traditional and Emerging Themes in Jamaican Popular Music*, Ian Randle: Kingston, pp. 127–38.

Hahn, David (2020), personal interview, Detroit, 11 November.

Hawks, Harry (2013), 'Featured artist – Errol Thompson', *Reggae Collector*, https://www.reggaecollector.com/en/feature/artist.php?artist_id=693. Accessed 20 November 2019.

Heaps, Ira (2020), personal interview, Detroit, 12 August.

Hendley, David (2003), 'King Tubby', *Natty Dread*, Academia, http://www.academia.edu/7877998/KING_TUBBY_by_Dave_Hendley._1st_published_June_2003_in_the_French_magazine_Natty_Dread. Accessed 25 January 2019.

Henriques, Julian (2003), 'Sonic dominance and the reggae sound system session', *The Auditory Culture Reader*, Oxford: Berg.

Henriques, Julian (2008), *Sonic Bodies: The Skills and Performance Techniques of the Reggae Sound System Crew*, London: Goldsmiths.

Henriques, Julian (2011), *Sonic Bodies: Reggae Soundsystems, Performance Techniques, and Ways of Knowing*, New York: Continuum Books.

Herman, Chin Loy (1975), *Aquarius Dub*, Kingston , JA: Aquarius.

Hitchins, Ray (2014), *Vibe Merchants: The Sound Creators of Jamaican Popular Music*, Farnham:Ashgate.

Hitchins, Ray (2018), personal interview, The University of the West Indies, JA, 2 October.

Holmes, Thom (2002), *Electronic and Experimental Music: Pioneers in Technology and Composition*, New York: Routledge.

References

Hope, Donna (2018), personal interview, The University of the West Indies, 3 December.

Hutton, Clinton (2018), 'A history of dub music', *Guisse Clarke Dub Anthology*, liner notes, CD, Kingston, JA: Anchor Music Works.

Ihde, Don (2007), *Listening and Voice: Phenomenologies of Sound*, Albany, NY: State University of New York.

Impact All Stars (1973), *Java, Java, Java, Java*, Kingston, JA: Impact.

James, Lloyd (2019), 'King Jammy', *Dub Conference*, University of the West Indies, Kingston, Jamaica, 15 February.

Katz, David (2000), *People Funny Boy: The Genius of Lee 'Scratch' Perry*, Edinburgh: Payback Press.

Katz, David (2012), *Solid Foundation: An Oral History of Reggae*, London: Jawbone.

Katz, David (2013), 'In search of the first dub LP', Red Bull Music Academy, 7 October, http://daily.redbullmusicacademy.com/2013/10/first-dub-lp-in-search-of. Accessed 1 December 2018.

Katz, David (2014a), 'A history of mute beat', Red Bull Music Academy, https://daily.redbullmusicacademy.com/2014/10/mute-beat-feature. Accessed 15 October 2014.

Katz, David (2014b), 'War ina Tokyo: The curious world of Japan's reggae scene', *FactMag*, https://www.factmag.com/2014/11/24/war-ina-tokyo-the-curious-world-of-japans-reggae-scene/3/. Accessed 24 November 2014.

Katz, David (2015), 'A beginner's guide to King Tubby, the producer who turned dub into an art form', *FactMag*, https://www.factmag.com/2015/05/19/king-tubby-beginners-guide-dub-reggae/. Accessed 25 January 2019.

Katz, David (2019), personal interview, Detroit, 5 December.

Katz, David (n.d.), 'The Ariwa/Mad Professor story', https://www.ariwa.com/ariwa-story. Accessed 11 October 2019

Kush, Kayla (2018), 'Women in reggae – Patricia Chin aka Miss Pat of VP Records', *Rootfire*, https://rootfire.net/women-in-reggae-patricia-chin-aka-miss-pat-of-vp-records/ Accessed November 2018.

Mann, Larisa Kingston (2018), 'Rude citizenship: Jamaican musical challenges to copyright(ed) culture', *The Quietus*, 17 October, https://thequietus.com/articles/25494-music-copyright-jamaica%20dub?curator=MusicREDEF. Accessed 17 October 2018.

Matthews, David (2018), *Voices of the Windrush Generation: The Real Story Told by the People Themselves*, London: Blink Publishing.

Mayseles, Phillip (2002), 'Dubbing the nation', *Small Axe*, 11 March, pp. 91–111.

McClure, Steve (1995), 'Nippon, Tachyon make reggae deals', *Billboard*, 15 July, https://books.google.co.uk/books?id=ygsEAAAAMBAJ&pg=PA41&lpg=PA41&dq=McClure,+Steve+(1995),+%E2%80%98Nippon,+Tachyon+make+reggae+deals%E2%80%99+billboard&source=bl&ots=bau9Rvqljz&sig=ACfU3U3mfKwvUXxTUNluci-6uO8GRNR7moA&hl=en&sa=X&redir_esc=y#v=onepage&q=McClure%2C%20Steve%20(1995)%2C%20%E2%80%98Nippon%2C%20Tachyon%20make%20reggae%20deals%E2%80%99%20billboard&f=false. Accessed 5 December 2020.

McLuhan, Marshall (1964), *Understanding Media: The Extensions of Man*, Cambridge: MIT Press.

Meyers, Tony (2018), personal interview, Kingston, 3 October.

Millard, Andre (2005), *America on Record: A History of Recorded Sound*, Cambridge: Cambridge University Press.

Niaah, Sonjah Stanley (2018), personal interview, The University of West Indies, JA, 2 October.

Nugent, Jayson (2020), personal interview, Detroit, 10 August.

Oliver, Rowan (2017), 'In dub conference: Empathy, groove, and technology in jamaican popular music', in E. King and C. Waddington (eds), *Music and Empathy*, Washington: Routledge, pp. 194–208.

Partridge, Christopher H. (2010), *Dub in Babylon: Understanding the Evolution and Significance of Dub Reggae in Jamaica and Britain from King Tubby to Post-punk*, London: Equinox.

Perry, Lee 'Scratch' (2019), personal interview, Chicago, 20 September.

Prince Buster's Allstars (1972), *The Message Dubwise*, Kingston, JA: Prince Buster Music.

Rachel, Daniel (2016), *Walls Come Tumbling Down: The Music and Politics of Rock Against Racism, 2 Tone, and Red Wedge*, London: Picador.

Schenck, Rob (2019), 'Land of the rising dread: Five decades of sound system culture in Japan, http://www.dub-stuy.com/land-of-the-rising-dread/. Accessed 23 August 2019

Sherwood, Adrian (2019), personal interview, Detroit, 19 September.

References

The Skatalites (2018), 'History', Alpha Boys School Radio, http://www.alphaboysschoolradio.com/roll-call-2.html. Accessed 1 December 2018.

Sterling, Marvin D. (2010), *Babylon East: Performing Dancehall, Roots Reggae, and Rastafari in Japan*, Durham and London: Duke University Press.

Sterling, Marvin D. (2011), 'Toward an analysis of global blackness: Race, representation, and jamaican popular culture in japan', in Y. Takezawa (ed.), *Racial Representations in Asia*, Kyoto: Kyoto University Press.

Steel Pulse (2019), 'About', https://steelpulse.com/about. Accessed 14 August 2019.

Sterne, Jonathan (2003), *The Audible Past: Cultural Origins of Sound Reproduction*, Durham: Duke Univesity Press.

Stolzoff, Norman C. (2000), *Wake the Town and Tell the People: Dancehall Culture in Jamaica*, Durham and London: Duke University Press.

Sullivan, Paul (2014), *Remixology: Tracing the Dub Diaspora*, London: Reaktion.

Surico, John (2015), 'How the gangs of 1970s New York came together to end their wars', *Vice*, http://vice.com/en_us/article/kwxwzv/how-the-gns-of-1970s-new-york-came-together-to-end-their-wars-618. Accessed 18 June 2015.

Taylor, Angus (2019), 'Interview - Sylvan Morris at Studio 1', *Reggaeville*, 1 April, https://www.reggaeville.com/artist-details/sylvan-morris/news/view/interview-sylvan-morris-at-studio-1/. Accessed 18 June 2021.

Toop, David (2008), 'Replicant: On dub', in C. Cox and D. Warner (eds), *Audio Culture: Readings in Modern Music*, New York: Continuum, pp. 355–57.

Turino, Thomas (2008), *Music as Social Life: The Politics of Participation*, Chicago: University of Chicago Press.

The Upsetters (1973), *Upsetters 14: Blackboard Jungle/Blackboard Jungle Dub*, Kingston, JA: Upsetters Records.

VanPelt, Carter (2019), *Down in Jamaica: 40 Years of VP Records*, liner notes, May, New York: VP Records.

Veal, Michael (2007), *Dub: Soundscapes and Shattered Songs in Jamaican Reggae*, Middletown, CT: Wesleyan University Press.

Vendrys, Thomas (2015), 'Versions, dubs, and riddims: Dub and the transient dynamics of Jamaican music', *Dancecult: Journal of Electronic Dance Music Culture*, 7:2, pp. 5–24.

Ware, Evan (2015), *Their Ways: Theorizing Reinterpretation in Popular Music*, Ph.D. Dissertation, Michigan: University of Michigan.

Warnett, Gary (2016), 'How the Block Party invented hip hop', *The Daily*, July, https://www.mrporter.com/en-us/daily/how-the-block-party-invented-hip-hop/1098. Accessed 7 July 2019.

Warwick, Oli (2018), 'Dubbing is a must: The modern sound of leftfield dub', https://www.factmag.com/2018/01/28/leftfield-dub-seekers-bokeh-boomarm/. Accessed 28 January 2018.

Warwick, Oli (2019), 'Even the earth gets dizzy: The career and collaborations of Ari Up', Red Bull Music Academy, https://daily.redbullmusicacademy.com/2019/06/ari-up-the-slits-feature. Accessed 7 August 2019.

Whitfield, Gregory Mario (2003), 'The Adrian Sherwood interview: The On-U sound experience, the On-U sound family', *Uncarved*, http://www.uncarved.org/dub/onu/onu.html. Accessed 15 August 2019.

Williams, Phillip (2018), '10 essential UK reggae and dub albums', Red Bull Music Academy, https://www.redbull.com/gb-en/essential-uk-reggae-dub-albums. Accessed 21 May 2018.

Williams, Raymond (1976), *Keywords: A Vocabulary of Culture and Society*, Oxford: Oxford University Press.

Williams, Sean (2012), 'Tubby's dub style: The live art of record production', in S. Frith and S. Zagorski-Thomas (eds), *The Art of Record Production: An Introductory Reader for a New Academic Field*, Ashgate Popular and Folk Music Series, Farnham: Ashgate Publishing, pp. 235–46.

Wilner, Brandon (2020), '40 years later reggae's heart still beats in the Bronx', *New York Times*, https://www.nytimes.com/2020/01/05/arts/music/wackies-reggae-lloyd-barnes.html. Accessed 15 September 2019.

Wilson, Tim (n.d.), 'The complete force: Wackies, a primer', *The Ransom Note*, https://www.theransomnote.com/music/interviews/the-complete-force-wackies-a-primer/. Accessed 1 October 2019.

Young, Alex (2008), 'Dusting em off: Augustus Pablo – King Tubby meets rockers uptown', *Consequence of Sound*, 28 December, https://consequence.net/2008/12/dusting-em-off-augustus-pablo-king-tubby-meets-rockers-uptown/. Accessed 18 June 2021.

About the Author

Eric Abbey, Ph.D., is a professor of English and literature at the Oakland Community College in Michigan. He is the co-editor of *Hardcore, Punk, and Other Junk: Aggressive Sounds in Contemporary Music* (2014), published by Lexington Books, and the author of *Garage Rock and Its Roots: Musical Rebels and the Drive for Individuality* (2006), published by McFarland Books. He is a professional musician with the groups, J. Navarro & the Traitors, Detroit Riddim Crew, Killer Diller and 1592, a producer of ska and reggae, and owner of Abbey Productions, LLC. Abbey also works producing dub riddims and tracks for musicians around the world and owns Pocket Sound System. His continuing work focuses on dub and recording strategies in Jamaica.

Index

100 decibels 125
18 Dromilly Avenue 72
2-Tone 59, 99
24-track 30, 31
45 rpm xv, 85, 97
4th Street Orchestra 94
555 Dub Street 78, 84
85 Sherwood Crescent 82

A

A-side 44, 73, 84, 88, 104, 141, 152
Abraham, Alfred 114
ACES 16 96
acetate xix, 18, 72, 95
Adams, Glen 44, 113, 124
Adorno 41, 59, 61
African Head Charge 97, 107, 141
African Skank 48, 49
Afrika Bambaataa 113, 118, 138
After the Rain 142
After Tonight 95
Ah Weh 101, 105
Al Capone 55
All for Free 122
Alpha Blondy 95
Alpha Boys School 4, 26, 57

Alphonso, Roland 56
amp 74
Ampex 96
Ampex 1100 100
Ampex MM1000 111
amplifiers xxiv, 7, 80
Anderson, Gladstone 44, 56
Answer 10, 13
Anthony Red Rose 82
Antibalas 125, 126
Apache 117
Apeman Skank 48, 52
Aquarius Dub 17, 18, 21, 22, 23, 30, 31, 32, 33, 36, 42, 53, 58, 150, 157
Aquarius Records 31
Aquizim 96
Argentinian 97
Ari Up 129
Ari Up and the True Warriors 129
Ariwa 96
Asamoto, Hirofumi 141
Aswad 89, 100
atmosphere 44
atoms 41, 42, 156
attunement 4, 157

173

audible xvi, xxv, 27, 155

audience xx, xxv, 11, 19, 25, 26, 33, 37, 42, 47, 65, 76, 78, 81, 87, 98, 136, 153, 155

auditory 22

autonomy 40, 59

auxiliary percussion 27, 49, 122

Axelrod, Victor aka Tiklah 125, 126

B

b-boy 112, 119

B-side xx, 2, 3, 5, 48, 50, 67, 72, 73, 84, 85, 88, 97, 103, 122, 123, 127, 141, 151

Ba Ba Boom 7

Baby I Love You So 73

Bachelard, Gaston 60, 61, 68

Back to Black 126

Baker, Jeff aka King Django 131

Bananarama 95

Bantu 123

Barnes, Lloyd 109, 110–13, 119, 124, 127, 129, 155

Barrett, Aston 44

Barrett, Aston 'Family Man' 73

Barrett, Carlton 73

Basic Channel 119

bass resonance xxii

bass-heavy 49

bedroom producer 74

Beethoven 42

Bennet, Val 56

Big Knob 75, 84, 85

Big Youth 3, 66, 68, 112

'Big Youth' (song) 57, 68

Bim Sherman 97

Bim Skala Bim 97

Birmingham, England 92

Black Ark 44, 46, 47, 86, 91, 110

Black Cats 118

Black Harem 57, 65, 66

Black Jack 113

Black Liberation Dub

Black Man's Dub 19, 29

Black Panta 48

Black Scorpio 12

Black Sounds of Freedom xxiv

Black Spades 117, 118

Black Uhuru xxiv

Blackbeard 91, 95, 101

Blackboard Jungle Dub 40, 42, 43–45, 48, 53, 54, 58, 74, 150, 154

Blackbyrd 120, 124

Blackman, Paul 85

Blackwell, Chris 7

bleed over 25

Blood and Fire 125

Blue Beat 56, 100

Blue Beat records 63

Blue Diamonds 118

blues xxiii, xxv, 63, 151

Boasy Tuesday 153

Bob Marley and the Wailers xxvii, 7, 116

Bogdanovich, Josef 151

Bokeh Versions 106, 152

Boma-ya-Dub 120

Bongo Pat 83

boogie-woogie 56

Bovell, Dennis 91, 94, 95, 96, 99, 100, 101, 103, 105, 106

Brace a Boy 84

Braces Tower Dub 73

Brad's Record Den 113, 117

Brazilian 97

break boy 112

break section 112

breakbeat 89

Brenner, Dan 110, 125, 126, 127

British 55, 89, 90, 92, 93, 94, 98, 106, 138, 148

Bronxdale houses 118

Brooks, Baba 56

Brother Louie (Hot Chocolate) 95

Brown Sugar 91

Brown, Dennis 28, 30, 34, 115, 116

Brown, Hopeton 'Scientist' 1, 7, 82

Brown, James 97, 150

Brown, Selwyn 93

bubbles 51, 122, 147

Bucky Skank 48

Bullwackie 109, 110, 123

BullWackie's All Stars 119

Burning Spear 101, 116

burru xxv, 144

Bustamante, Alexander 45

Buster Wild Bells 63

Buster's Boop Boop Beat 63

Butterfly 141

Byles, Junior 46, 49

Byron Lee and the Dragonaires 59

C

Cabaret Voltarie 98

call-outs 10

calypso 21, 109, 114

Campbell, Cecil Bustamante 55, 56

Campbell, Clive 112, 113

Capo, Thompson 125

Carib Gems 97

Caribbean 89, 90, 109, 116, 139

Carol Grimes 94, 100

Caveman Skank 52

Channel One 7, 8, 131

Cheating Dub 19, 25

Chin-Loy, Herman 18, 30, 31, 153

Chin, Clive 17, 19, 21, 22, 37, 114, 153

Chin, Patricia 115

175

Chin, Vincent 'Randy' 114, 115
chucka 26, 29, 49
Chung, Geoffrey 30
Chung, Mikey 30
Cimarons 89, 92, 93, 100
Clapton, Eric 93
Clark Kent 113
Clarke, Augustus 'Gussie' 12, 14
clavinet 72, 73
Cliff, Jimmy 92
Clocktower Records 73, 113, 114, 155
Coffia 142, 143
Coke La Rock 112, 113
Collins, Ansell 30
commodity 11, 31, 32, 40, 41, 42, 53, 59, 69
Communism 20
compression 33
conga(s) 33, 34, 49, 121
conservative 20, 45
consumer 11, 156
copyright xx, 1
Corner Crew Dub 73, 85
Count Ossie 63
cowbell 65, 66, 67, 68
Crazy Baldhead 125, 127, 131, 152
Creary, Benbow 44
Creation Rebel 97
Cuba 20

Cultural Dub 7
cultural production xiv
culture industry 40
Cut after Cut 101, 102, 103
cymbal(s) 18, 32, 33
cymbal splash 32

D

Dammers, Jerry 99
dance-hall 10, 63, 68, 136, 137, 153
Danny, Dane and Lorraine 64
Davies, Sister Mary Ignatius 4
Deadly Dragon Sound 134, 148
decomposition 43
delay processor 102, 157
deletions 40
Democratic Socialism 20, 45
DI 111
Digidub 130
digital delay 102
Dillinger 51, 84
Dis-Ya-a-Dub 120, 123
Disciples 106
DJ Kool Herc 109, 112, 118, 119
DJ Mario 118
DMX 141, 142, 143, 145, 146, 147
Dodd, Clement 'Coxsone' xviii, 6, 21, 46, 59, 69
Dollar in the Teeth 44
Douglas, Val 30

Down Sound records 151
Down Town 48
Dreamland Skank 48, 50
drum and bass (genre) 89
Drum Call 120, 121
Drum Rock 48, 50
Drummond, Don 4
Dry and Heavy 134
Dub Conference: Winston Edwards & Blackbeard at 10 Downing Street 91
Dub is a Weapon 125, 126, 127, 152
Dub machine 73
Dub Me Crazy 96
Dub Organiser 48, 51
Dub Serial 6
Dub Side of the Moon 125
Dub Store 152
Dub Stuy 168
Dub Syndicate 97
Dub You Can Feel 74
Dub-Stuy 139
dubplate(s) xix, xxi, 7, 11, 12, 18, 22, 79, 95
dubstep 106, 152
Dubwise: Morris on Dub 7
Duffus, Chenley 51
Duke Reid 21, 62, 111
Dunbar, Sly 44
Dunhaney Park 82

Dunn, Franklyn 92
Dynamic Sounds 58, 72, 75
Dynamics 57, 63, 93

E

E.T. Special 19, 26
Each One Dub 73, 83
Each One Teach One 83
Earthquake 106
Eastern 58
Easy Star All Stars 125
Eccles, Clancy 46
echo 48, 50, 74, 80, 141, 142, 157
Echo's Song 142, 144
editing xix, 36, 77, 79, 121
electronic engineer xxiv
electronic music xv, xxiv, 74, 106
Elephant Man 114
Elephant Rock 48, 49
Ellis, Alton 30
Ellis, Bobby 73
Ellis, Maurice 92
Emch 152
EQ 11
Ernie B's 131, 155
ET 24

F

faders 3, 24, 30, 67, 76
Fairclough, Osmond Theodore 45

177

Fairlight 5
False Rasta 84
Far East 67, 132
Farrell, Perry 97
Federal 63, 93, 111
Fever 48, 50, 52
Firehouse 82
Fishmans 134, 152
floating 58, 64, 78, 103, 120
Folkes Brothers 63
Foreman, George 123
foundation riddims xviii, 3, 9, 10, 13, 127
four-track xx, 47
framework 15, 20, 50, 65
France 107
Fraser, Neil Joseph Stephen 96, 97, 149, 150
Free for All 119, 120, 122, 123, 124, 125
Freeman, Jeremy 134, 148
frequency xvi, xvii, 11, 32, 40, 75
Frozen Dub 73, 86
full-length records xv, 14
Fullwood, Fully 19

G

Gabbidon, Basil 93
Gardiner, Boris 44
Ghetto Brothers 117
Gibbs, Joe 6, 24

Gichie, Locksley 92
Glazer, Max 110, 125, 126, 152
Glory Stompers 118
Goats Head Soup 59
Goosebury 94, 101
Gordon, Ken 'Fatman' 141
Gordon, Ralhus 'Raleigh' 46
Gordon, Vin 4
Gordon, Vincent 'Don D Junior' 73
Grammy Award 93
Grand Groove Records 113
Grand Theft Auto IV 126
Grandmaster Flash 112, 138
Greensleeves xxiv, 116, 125
Gregg, Sheldon 126
grime 89, 106, 152
groove music 61, 157
Guiding Dub 19, 25, 28, 153
gunshots xxiii, 48
Gyptian 114, 132

H

Hackney 93
Hahn, Dave 110, 125, 126, 127
Haile Selassie I 20
Haines, Jerry 56
Haiti 109
Half Way Tree 31
Hall, Richard 'Dirty Harry' 73
Hammond, Beres 114

Index

hand drum 67
Handsworth Revolution 92, 93
Harmon mute 144
harmony 31
Harper, Raymond 56
Harris, Jerry 119
Harry J's 6, 7
Heaps, Ira 127, 128, 129, 130, 131, 158
Heavy Duty 31
Hell's Angels 117, 131
Heptones 7, 86, 116
Herculords 113
Hevalo 112
Hi-Fidelity Dub Sessions: Roots Combination 126
Hibbert, Frederick 'Toots' 46
Hide Away Dub 19, 29
high-pass filter 18, 24, 27, 32, 74, 75, 83, 86
Hinds, David 93
hip-hop xv, xxvii, 109, 138, 139
Holt, Flabba 8
Holt, John 6, 122
homemade 78, 87
Horkheimer 59
House of Blues 126
house parties 21, 90, 109
Hudson, Keith 91, 101, 106
Hunt, Clive 'Azul' 119

Hunter, Dave 101
Hyperdub 106

I

I Man 30, 33, 153
I Wah Dub 95
I Will Never Let You Go 10
Imai, Hideyuki 141
Impact All Stars 18, 19, 46
Impact! 22, 46
Imperial Jay Cee 113
In Time 92
Indonesia 107
Island Music 21
Island Records 92
Island Records UK 106
isomorphic 9, 10
Ites of Dub 101, 104

J

Jabba 126
Jah 9 xiii, 15, 97, 132
Jah Bunny 91, 101
Jah Jah Dub 31, 35
Jah Rock 153
Jah Shaka 106
Jah Sufferer 95
Jah Warrior 106
Jam 1 12
Jam One 153
Jamaican Labour Party 20, 45

James Brown and his Famous Flames 150

James, Lloyd 'King Jammy' 82

Jamiroquai 97

Jammy's Records xxiv

Jammyland 127–31, 155, 158

Japan xiii, xiv, xxi, 97, 132–42, 146–48, 151–53, 154

Japanese 97, 134–42, 146–48, 151, 157

Japansplash 134, 140

Java Dub 19, 28

Java Plus 57, 67

Java, Java, Java, Java 17, 19, 21–24, 26, 29, 31, 33, 36, 42, 53, 58, 150

jazz 51, 67, 114, 125, 139, 142, 143, 144

jazz structure 26

Jet Black 57, 65

JLP 20, 21, 45, 46

Joe Gibbs & the Professionals 6

Joe's Pub 131

John III 131

Johnson, Jerry 119

Johnny Rotten 89, 152

Johnson, Linton Kwesi 94

Jones, Brian 94

Jones, Euton 'Fergus' 101

Jones, Hedley xvii

Judge Dread 55

jukeboxes 115

Jumping Jack 31, 35

jungle 89

Jungle Fever 48, 52

Jungle Jim 48, 50

Jungle Rock 31, 36

Junior Delahaye 119

Junko 137, 148

K

Kasha Skank 48

Kaya Skank 48, 52, 153

Keep on Moving 51

keyboard 19, 28, 29, 45–47, 91–93, 101–05, 141–46

kick drum 29, 35, 102, 103, 106, 120, 122

King (Prince) Jammy xxiv, 7, 75, 134

King Addies 112

King Babylon Dub 19

King of Babylon 46

King Tubby xxi, xxii, xxv, xxvi, 6, 7, 13, 37, 42, 44, 45, 54, 71–96, 126, 150, 153, 156

King Tubby Meets Rockers Uptown 13, 81, 87, 150, 152, 154

King, Carole 34

Kodama, Kazumi 'Echo' 141

Kode9 107

Konders, Bobby 110, 126

Kpiaye, John 91

Kuti, Fela 95

L

L.A. 126

lacquer 73

Lamont, Eric 'Biggy Bunnny' 27

Lee, Bunny 72

Lee, Byron 7, 14, 58, 59

Lee, Carlton 18, 32, 57–59, 64, 67, 69, 153

Levy, Carl 92

Levy, Douglas 119

Lewis, Alva 44

Limousine 94

Lindo, Earl 'Wire' 30

Lion 82

Lloyd Charmer's the Now Generation 30

loop 74

Love Crisis xxiv

Love Won't Come Easy 86

Lover's Rock 88, 91, 94, 96, 142

Lovers Skank 48, 51

low-pass filter xxiii, 153

Luciano 82, 131

Lyn Taitt and the Jets 65

Lynn, Robbie 30

M

Mad Professor 96, 97, 101, 106, 148–51

Madness 55

Maka 95

Mamba/Atra 92

Mango 73, 85

Manley, Michael 20, 45, 54

Manley, Norman 45

Marley, Bob xxvi, xxvii, 7, 8, 40, 44, 46, 57, 92, 115, 116, 134, 137, 140

Martin, Alphonso 93

Mass Manipulation 93

Massive Attack 97

Massive B Soundsystem 126

Masta Simon 151

Masui, Akihito 141

Mathews, Winston 91

Matsuaga, Takayoshi 141

Matterhorn, Tony 112, 151

Matthias, Nathaniel 'Jerry' 46

Matumbi 89, 94, 95, 100, 101, 106, 125, 141

MC 27, 32, 37, 112, 136, 140

McCook, Tommy 4, 19, 26, 56, 57

MCI 5, 6, 72, 75, 79, 94, 95, 113, 155

MCI JH-400 6

McQueen, Ronald 93

Meditation Dub 120, 124

Meet Me at the Corner 28

Meet Me Dub 19, 28

Mellotron 94

melodica 19, 28, 49, 57, 67, 72, 73, 83–86, 92, 142, 147

Melodisc 56, 63

mento xxv, 21, 45

Meyer, Tony 56

Mighty Crown 134, 136, 137, 148, 151, 155

Mighty Massa 134

Mighty Massa Soundsystem 134

Mikey Dread 97

Miller, Jacob 82–85, 88

Mint Ah Music 101

Miss Pat 115

Mississippi 57, 65

Miyazaki, Izumi 'Dub Master X' 141

Modern (time period) 42

Mojito Mondays 153

Montego Bay 151

Moog 111

Moore, Johnny 'Dizzy' 4

Mooving Skank 48, 51, 153

More Cut/EMI 95

Morgan Heritage 114

Morgan, Derrick 58–59

Morris, Sylvan 6–8, 24, 153

Muhammad Ali 123

Munchi and the Corner Crew 123

Mundell, Hugh 83, 85

Mute Beat 134, 139–41, 147, 148, 155

Mutt and Jeff 4

MV Empire Windrush 89

N

Nation of Islam 118

National Front 93, 99

Native American 117

Natty Locks Dub 91

Nebuchadnezzar 46

Negril 129

Nelson, Junior 56

Netherlands 107

New Orleans 146

New York City xxiii, 109–32, 155

Nice Up 152

Nine Inch Nails 98

Ninja 134, 151

Nippon Columbia 140

No Problem 142, 145

Noise New York 128

north shore 20, 21

Notting Hill 90

Notting Hill Carnival 90

Nugent, Jayson 110, 125, 127, 131

Nyabinghi xxv, 63, 121

Nyah Time 31, 36

O

Ocampo, Eddie 125–26

Ocho Rios 151

Index

Oh Carolina 63

On-U Sound 91, 97, 98, 148

One Step Beyond 55

Osborne, Brad 113

Overheat 134, 140, 141

P

Pablo, Agustus 11, 19, 28, 30, 72, 73, 77, 81, 83, 85, 86, 92, 114, 147, 152

Parks, Arkland 'Drumbago' 56

Parks, Lloyd 46

Parliament 20, 45

Patois 135–37

Patricia 114, 115

Peckham 96

People's National Party 20, 45

Perry, Lee 'Scratch' xxi–xxvi, 12, 39–54, 58, 64, 97, 115, 125, 126, 141, 152, 153, 156

Pham, Quoc 152

Pharaoh Hiding 46

Phillips, Peter 45

Pick a Dub 91, 92

Pink Panther 153

Pithecan records 141

Pitterson, Karl 92

Place Called Africa 49

PNP 20, 45, 46

Polydemic 126

Pop Goes the Weasel 50

Prince Buster 55–69, 110, 111

Prince Buster All Stars 56

Prince Far-I 91

R

Rainbow 99

Randy's 19, 21, 22, 24, 46, 73, 77, 81, 93, 99, 114–16

Randy's Studio 17 21

Ranglin, Earnest 56

Rankin Taxi 134

RAR's Greatest Hits 100

Ras Menelik 119

Ras Takashi 132

Rastafarianism 20, 80

Rastafarians 63

Rastaman Vibration 7

Rebel Chase 101, 102, 104

Red Bull Radio 152

Reedy, Winston 92

Reggae Sumfest 151

Reggae Workshop 7

Rest Yourself 30

Return of Django 44

RG Jones 94, 95

Rice, Victor 125

Richards, Michael 'Boo' 30

Richards, Mikey 44

Ricky Trooper 153

Riddim Chango 134, 139

183

Riley, Mykaell 93, 98
River to Bank 101, 104
RJR Studios 63
Rock Against Racism 89, 93, 94, 98–100
Rod of Correction 46, 54
Rodriguez, Rico 56, 57
Rolling Stones 59
Roman Kings 117
Romeo, Max 24
Ronson, Mark 126
Roots Radics 8
Rotten, Johnny 85, 89, 152
Rough Signal 134
Ruddock, Leslie 'Stagga' 73
Ruddock, Osbourne 71, 72
Ruffin, Bruce 30
Ruggerio, Vic 129, 131
Rumbo Malt 30, 32, 33, 157

S

Sade 97
Saladin 57, 67
Salmon, Noel 91
Sammi T 151
Sangster, Donald 45
Sata A Masa Gana 57, 59, 67
Satta Dub 73, 86
Saunders, Red 98, 100
Savage Seven 118
Savage Skulls 117, 118
Say So 73, 85
Scientist 1, 7, 8, 82, 125
Scientist Wins the World Cup 125
scratching 112
Scully 72
Seaga, Edward 58, 61
Sean Paul 114
Sebastian, Tom 'The Great' 69
Shachtman, Noah 152
Shakespeare, Robbie 73
Shakespeare, Sly and Robbie 8
Shaking up Orange Street 55
Sham 69 92
Shearer, Hugh 46
Sherwood, Adrian 89, 91, 97, 98, 101, 106, 107, 141, 148
Sinead O'Connor 98
Singers and Players 97
Sisters of Mercy 4
Sizzla 82
ska xix, xx, xxiii, xxviii, 2, 4, 14, 21, 26, 32, 41, 45, 46, 55–57, 62, 63, 65, 89, 100, 101, 105, 107, 112, 125, 126, 142, 143, 156
Ska Be Doo Za 101
Skanking Dub 73, 76, 86
Skanking Easy 86
skinhead 92
Skinnerbox 125

Index

Smart, Leroy 4, 131
Smith, Conroy 82
Smith, Earl 'Chinna' 19, 44, 73
Smith, Slim 10
Social Democracy 20
Soho 94
Soon Come 125–27, 152
soul music 21
Soul Vendors 86
Soulful Dub 19, 26
Soundcraft 95, 96
Soundview 118
South London 96
Space Age 120
Spain 107
Spaker, Jay 152
specials 7, 12, 59, 81
Specials (band) 100
spring reverb 66, 74, 85
Stalag 14
Steel Pulse 89, 92, 93, 98, 100, 106
steppers 102, 103, 105, 106, 130, 142
Sterling, Keith 45
Sterling, Lester 4
Stick by Me 66
stick lead 25, 27, 32–36, 49, 65, 67, 104
Still Echo 141
Still Echo 141, 142, 146

Still Echo (melodica mix) 142, 147
Stone Love 12, 153
Stop Them Jah 73, 83
street dances 21
Strictly Dub Wize 95, 101
Strive 136
Stubborn All Stars 125
Studio 17 19, 21, 24, 114, 115, 116
Studio Abo 141
Studio One xviii, 6, 7, 24, 93
Sugar Minott 82
Summerfest Productions Limited 151
Summertime-Frozen Sun 142
Sunsplash 151
Swing Low 57, 66, 67

T

T-Ski Valley 113
Tachyon 134, 140
Takakura, Hiroshi 139
Taurus 82
Tell Me What I Did Wrong 151
Tempus 95, 101
Thatcher, Margaret 100
The Amazing Bert 113
the Aggrovators 73
the Barge 96
the Beastie Boys 97
the Black Panthers 118
the Clash 100

185

the Dirty Ones 117
the Downbeat 21
the Fall 98
the Heptones 7, 86, 116
the Hurricanes 49
the Jamaicans 7
The Man in Me 95
the Maytals 3, 46, 57
The Message 57, 64
The Message Dubwise 13, 56–64, 68, 69, 142, 150, 151, 152, 154, 157
the Mighty Two 24
the Orb 97
the Ruts DC 97
the Savage Nomads 117
the Skatalites 14, 26, 57, 142
the Slackers 125, 127
the Slits 95, 98
the Specials 100
the Tomahawks 117
The Trojan 21
the Wailers xxvii, 7, 44, 50–52, 92, 116
Thompson, Errol xxi, xxv, 6–8, 19, 24, 27, 37, 73, 153
Thompson, Linval 124
Thornton Heath 96
Ticklah Vs. Axelrod 126
Tiklah 125, 126, 152
Tilbury 89

Time Boom X De Devil Dead 97
To Be A Lover 51
toaster 27
Toasting xxvii, 112
Tosh, Peter xxvi, 57, 92, 115, 116
Totally Dubwise 106
Trafalgar Square 93
Treasure Isle 7, 94
Tribal Dub 120, 122
Tribal War 122
Trinidad and Tobago 89
Trojan Records 92, 95, 96, 106
Try Me 151
Tubby's Hometown Hi-Fi 72, 79, 80
Tubin, Brett 110
Tuff Gong 8, 140, 141
Twilight Zone 112
Two-Tone 89, 98, 100, 107
two-track xx, 6, 64, 72, 74, 150, 157

U

U-Roy 3, 12, 81, 112
Uk Garage 106
United Kingdom 89, 90–97, 101, 106, 107
Upsetters 14 Dub 44
Upsettrs 14 - Dub Blackboard Jungle 45
Uptown Mondays 153

Index

V

V/S Panta Rock 48

Van Pelt, Carter 109, 114, 125, 126

Vance, Tommy 152

vibraslap 86

Virgin 96

Voice of the People 55, 62, 63, 69

VP Records 114, 155

Vulcan 92

W

Wackie's 109, 110, 114, 117–32, 141, 142, 155

Wailer, Bunny 57, 140

Walker, Bagga 101

Wallace, Leroy 'Horsemouth' 4

Wash Wash 55

Washington Gardens 47

Water Pump 52

Waterhouse xxiv, 72, 81, 82

Weather Underground 118

Weddy Weddy Wednesdays 153

Wellpack band 91

West Indies 21, 101

West Indies Recording Limited 58

Westmoreland 1299

Wet Dream 24

White Plains 111, 113, 118

Whitehorse Lane 97

Who Say Jah No Dread 83

Whopping Thursdays 153

Why am I Treated so Bad 57, 65

Williams, Raymond xiii

Wilson, Delroy 7, 66

Windrush generation 90

Winehouse, Amy 126

WIRL 58

World War II 89

Wright, Winston 19

X

X-ray Spex 93, 100

Y

Yellowman 116

You Can Run 49

Yucky Skank 48

www.ingramcontent.com/pod-product-compliance
Lightning Source LLC
Chambersburg PA
CBHW071819230426
43670CB00013B/2499